The 72 Angels

Instant Access to The Angels of Power

DAMON BRAND

THE GALLERY OF MAGICK

Copyright © 2015 Damon Brand

All Rights Reserved. This book may not be reproduced, in whole or in part, in any form or by any means electronic or mechanical, including photocopying, recording, or by any information storage retrieval system now known or hereafter invented, without written permission from the publisher, The Gallery of Magick.

Disclaimer: Consider all information in this book to be speculation and not professional advice, to be used at your own risk. Damon Brand and The Gallery of Magick are not responsible for the consequences of your actions. Success depends on the integrity of your workings, the initial conditions of your life and your natural abilities, so results will vary. The information is never intended to replace or substitute for medical advice from a professional practitioner, and when it comes to issues of physical health, mental health or emotional conditions, no advice is given or implied, and you should always seek conventional, professional advice. The information is provided on the understanding that you will use it in accordance with the laws of your country.

CONTENTS

The Power of Angels	7
Decoding The Magick	9
The Secrets of Angelic Contact	10
How to Contact an Angel	12
The Force of Connection	14
The Angel of Universal Secrets	16
Singing to Angels	18
Preparing for Contact	19
Choosing an Angel	23
Crafting Your Request	25
Targeting Your Magick	28
Feeding the Angels	30
Pronunciation	32
Using The Sigil	35
Eleven Days of Angelic Contact	38
The Master Ritual	39
What is the Experience of Contact Like?	43
After the Ritual	46
Creating a Ritual	48
The 72 Angels of Magick	49
The Act of Choosing	194
Getting Involved with Your Magick	196
The Art of Letting Go	198
Doing Magick for Others	199
When Magick Works	200
Appendix A: The Master Ritual Simplified	201

The Power of Angels

When you contact the angels listed in this book, you will have the power to dominate success and fortune, obtain what you wish, protect yourself and stop enemies. These angels can be contacted easily, instructed directly and will gladly fulfill your desires. Summoning angels is said to be difficult, but there is a system that makes contact easy.

The 72 Angels of Magick is derived from my earlier books, *Magickal Angels* and *The Greater Magickal Angels*. If you have those books, you don't need this one. It's essentially the same material. In this book, however, there is a new talisman used to contact the angels, and all seventy-two angelic sigils have been updated with Hebrew, rather than Latin, with a modified method that makes contact easier. Don't worry, you don't need to be able to read a word of Hebrew – you just scan your eyes over the sigils.

The angels in this book can be contacted easily, and give you access to over a hundred powers that can improve your life. If you want to bring about safe, effective changes through magick, this is the best place to start.

This system has been developed over thirty years by a group of occultists known as The Gallery of Magick, with our aim being to create magick that works regardless of your religion or beliefs. The magick is not Jewish or Christian. Hebrew Psalms are used to contact the angels because they are shortcuts to angelic contact. There is a long tradition of using various verses and names to contact these angels. This book contains the words that work the best, and it has given us an extremely potent system. This magick is used by people of many religious backgrounds, and by atheists, and by those who just sense there is something magickal going on out there. The angels will respond to any strong desire, and help you bring about change in the world.

The angels in this book are known by many names, but most often they are called The Angels of the Shemhamphorasch. These angels can help you to develop and attract love, find harmony, increase fame, find strength, break through adversity, sleep well, heal yourself and obtain clear thought. There are angelic powers that enable you to invent, discover new methods, improve your business and find new supporters. You can free yourself of enemies and increase the loyalty of friends and lovers. The power to improve prosperity, win awards, write well, be stable, reduce anxiety, learn easily, understand in new ways and dominate strong personalities is at your hand. The angels can help you to excite new passion, discover more about yourself and see the past, present and future with clarity.

It is vital that you read the instructions thoroughly and take the work seriously. Although I encourage a playful confidence with magick, you should consider every magickal act a pact with reality. You are asking for magick to bring you a new reality, and you should be prepared to accept that reality.

Magick performed as a test to 'see if it works' will probably not work. You should find out what it is you want to change in your life, ensure that you understand the instructions in this book fully, and then commit to making that change through your own actions and with magick empowering your efforts.

This book also includes a method for empowering the talismans and sigils. This works even if you're using the sigils on a computer screen or other device. There is also information on how to choose an angel, as well as details on communicating directly with angels and developing relationships with them through your magick. Later in the book there is a section on performing angel magick for other people.

The angels in this book can help you to carry out difficult tasks, strengthen your will and increase your popularity. They can work to attract friendship, love, calm down arguments, keep lovers loyal and recover lost love. They will protect, uncover truth, stop liars and cheats, help you find work and increase your success in areas of fame and fortune. There are angels that can inspire artists and attract wealth, spreading the word about your work. Debtors can be made to pay up. You can turn enemies into friends, protect yourself from dangerous attacks, or lie low and remain unseen. Whether you are making deals, learning a trade, trying to pass exams or working to increase wealth, the angels can help. You can be popular with superiors, add power to all your work and to all your magick, and keep your willpower strong.

Whether you are seeking fame, money, wisdom or peace, the angelic powers can help you to improve your life in the ways that matter to you most. You don't need to believe anything or belong to any religion. The angels are ready to listen and ready to work for you. You don't need to be pure or worthy. All you need is a real desire; a strong desire for something to change in your world. If you have that desire, the angels will take you where you want to go. It is their job to give us the power to express the life we dream of living. All you have to do is ask in the right way.

Decoding The Magick

Just about all the magickal knowledge you need can be found on the internet, at no cost, and you can experiment for years trying to find out how to decode ancient grimoires. That's what we did and it worked for us, even though we had to buy old books and collect information gradually, as the internet wasn't available to us back in the seventies.

It took decades for us to realize some of our mistakes, and a lot of experimentation to find out what was really important in magick. Extensive research and access to private collections of magick led to great progress. There are countless theories and ideas going on out there, and finding something that works takes time. Our own work evolves continually, but there are several key secrets that make magick work. There is no better way to prove their power than to use them for angelic contact.

A great deal of the magickal knowledge on the internet is priceless, but there is a lot of disinformation and a lot of ideas, diagrams and images that simply don't work. You could spend a couple of hours Googling everything you need to know about angels, and you could even download a few free books – but they would be riddled with incorrect angelic names, false explanations of what the angels can do, and extremely long and difficult rituals. In many cases you wouldn't have the correct angelic seal, and you'd be using the wrong invocation to call them. There are people trying to contact angels using the very worst information, who then wonder why the magick isn't working.

The good news is that when you get these details right, angelic contact is instant. We have removed the misinformation, and given you the purest access to seventy-two angels of power. While it is true that many forms of magick can be used to contact angels, what's presented here is the method that we have found to work the most effectively, even if you are new to magick. These are angels that can bring you wealth, fame, protection and other powers such as the ability to uncover secrets, repel evil, discover more about your creativity or ease the pain of mental suffering. The magick may be simple, but its force is devastating.

The methods used in this book are easy to follow. It doesn't matter whether you believe in them, only that you act *as though* you believe in them. You can think of yourself as an actor putting on a play. So long as you go in to this system with that level of commitment, you will see results.

Using this simple system, you can get an angel's attention, talk to the angel directly, and let it make changes in your life.

The Secrets of Angelic Contact

To contact an angel all you need is its sigil (or seal), and its name. The sigil is a small diagram or drawing, and the name is something that should be repeated three times. Correct pronunciation is not essential, but we've supplied the best pronunciation for Western speakers.

Many occultists would agree that, in theory, the above is true. Angelic contact takes nothing more than desire, a name and a sigil. In practice, it helps if you add in some more directed ritual magick to ensure that contact is made.

There are many magickal approaches to obtaining angelic contact, and some require endless bathing and confession, meditation and purification. But that approach has always seemed over-the-top to me, because when you hear stories about angelic contact, angels help the poor, the lost and the dispossessed. Most stories of spontaneous angelic contact are about ordinary people, or the destitute and poor, or soldiers who are about to die in battle but are then rescued in a flash of light. Whatever angels may be, they do not dislike humans, and it is their sacred duty to help us when we ask.

I don't think we need to dress up and get clean to meet them. Angels don't see us as dirty annoyances. We are already worthy of their attention and they are ready to listen.

Other approaches to contact use prayer and faith and urge you to train yourself over months, straining and forcing yourself to believe the angel is there. Such approaches imply that you're going to have to try very hard to get the angels to hear you.

My experience has been that angels are always listening, and it doesn't take much effort to contact them. If you use a seal or sigil, an angelic name and some basic concentration, that may be all that's needed. Angels help the most miserable people and the lost, they help the greedy and the mean, they help the cruel and the cold. If somebody asks for help from an angel, help arrives.

Do not feel a need to bathe before speaking to them. Do not feel unworthy. Do not worry about whether your desire is 'right', or whether an angel will approve. You make the choice about what you want and you get to live with the result. The angels are there to enable you to perform your true will on earth. If you know what it is that you truly desire, it will come to pass.

Only you know what it is that you want from life, and your desires change and grow as you change and grow. Pay attention to your real desires, and do the things that make you happy and fulfilled.

I occasionally fly light airplanes, and I once met a pilot who had saved his money for years and spent months getting his license, but I could tell that – despite his assertion that he was going to buy a plane one day – he didn't really *like* flying. Somewhere in his life he'd convinced himself that being a pilot would make him happy, even though he had no real love of the *experience*. It was only when he could admit this to himself that he could let go of his false dream and find out what he really wanted. Then he was able to make a real improvement to his life.

Look for the experiences that make you happy. Look for the situations that make you able to express yourself and feel love for your journey through life.

To live a happy and fulfilled life, you need to find a balance between your animal desires and love, between material goods and pleasant experiences. This does not mean you need to seek a noble life. If you are at the point in your life where all you really want is a huge house to retire in, or enough money to travel, or to find new love – if that's what you really want, then that is fine. The angels don't judge.

The warning is given because the angels will provide what you ask for. Be careful what you ask for, because angelic power can be life-changing. Other forms of magick concentrate on small details, such as attracting some extra money, but angelic magick is likely to change an entire situation. The angels paint in broad strokes, so be certain you want the change you ask for.

And although angels can guide you, when you ask for their wisdom, they are not there to rule your life or tell you what to do with your time. You are responsible for your life, and it is up to you to find your desires and then fulfill them. Do not ask the angel to tell you what's best for you, because it is your job to find out what's best, and then use magick to bring about those circumstances.

The purpose of the magick is to change yourself and the world to get the results you want, so never put your life in the hands of another entity. Angels are messengers, and can give access to great wisdom, but they are not in charge of your life. Once you've received their wisdom, *you* get to decide what happens, and the angels will use their powers, and hosts of powers that work for them, to bring you the desired result.

In the following chapters I will reveal the secrets that make angelic contact possible and instantaneous. If you're familiar with magick, some of these ideas may be challenging, or they may seem familiar. If you are new to magick, the ideas may seem strange, but realize that this system was built by taking many successful magickal ideas – both ancient and modern - and refining them into something that works. The secrets may seem strange at times, but they bring this magick to life.

How to Contact an Angel

The next few chapters cover concepts and techniques that you will use to contact the angels, showing you exactly what to say and do, and how to raise up the powers of magick. Some of the techniques require you to read slowly and understand the concepts clearly, but you probably want to know *how to contact an angel*.

This chapter gives you a basic outline of how the overall process works.

Firstly, you will create and empower a unique talisman. This talisman will be used in every ritual, to give you access to the seventy-two angels.

You will then decide what result you want, and determine which angel or angels would be most suitable for the task.

You then plan and write out your request in detail and prepare to perform the ritual.

During the ritual you will use the angel's sigil. Each angel has a unique sigil that has been drawn inside a circle of power. This image ensures that contact is made, that you remain safe and that results will occur in the real world.

You use the talisman and the angelic sigil, combined with a series of words and names to attract the attention of the angel.

Once contact is made you speak your request and wait for any response from the angel. There may be none, or there may be a powerful response. Either way, the angel has heard.

You repeat the working for eleven days. The result will manifest.

Magick is only ever one factor in a situation, so the result may be instant or it may take three days, three weeks or three months for you to see results. This depends entirely upon what you're asking for and your current situation. If you ask for protection, it's instantaneous. If you ask to be more popular, it may take days. If you ask for wealth and fame, you can expect rapid changes that develop and last over several years.

Sometimes you only need one angel. At other times it's better to work with two or more angels on one problem.

Ideally you should deal with one task at a time, to ensure you maintain full concentration and commitment during the ritual. However, if you need to protect yourself, silence an enemy, find some money and make yourself popular all at the same time, it can be done, if you have the focus and time to work four complete rituals every day for eleven days. If there's no urgency, it's best to work on one problem at a time.

It can take some time to learn the techniques and ideas in this book, as well as practicing the pronunciations and getting familiar with the ritual approach. For some people, getting to grips with all these ideas and preparing the talisman and the sigils takes a couple of weeks. Others get to grips with it in a day and perform their first ritual straight after reading the instructions. Go with whatever approach feels right to you, but don't worry or overthink your magick.

The beauty of angelic magick is that once you put in the effort, contact is instant. The contact *will* be made. It is better to perform imperfect magick often, than to worry about every detail and avoid magick until you've set everything up perfectly. When you can, get on with the magick and get the changes you want to see in your life.

The book will also show you how to experience the presence of the angel. For some, this happens instantly and dramatically. For others, it can be a subtle sense of a presence. There are others who don't sense the angels at all, but still see the results. If you want to build a relationship with an angel, so that you can experience the contact directly, I'll show you the extra steps you can take.

Before describing the ritual itself, there are several powers and concepts that you need to become familiar with, and these will be described in the following chapters.

The Force of Connection

This book offers secrets of angelic contact that I have never seen used in combination elsewhere.

The first of these concerns the energy of lightning, or electricity. Magick is often concerned with the four 'elements' of earth, air, fire and water. They are used symbolically in many rituals. The fifth element is often referred to as spirit, or something similar.

We have found, however, that when you bring the power of electricity - the blue light that thunders from the sky - into your rituals, it forges an instant connection between you and the spirits. After all, lightning makes a visible connection between the heavens and the earth.

Occult literature is filled with spells and rituals that refer to lightning, and the word 'thunder' appears in sacred texts more often than you would suppose. Electricity, far from being a modern invention, is something the ancients used for angelic contact. It is the secret key that opens many magickal pathways.

Don't worry, you don't need to plug into any electrical power – this is done purely with words and imagination, but the power is as real as an electric shock.

Our brains are riddled with electrical charge, and when our thoughts are directed to imagine lightning, we connect with a host of angels. If you want to get an angel's attention, this is the way.

I should be clear that this process uses the imagination, so you should not be tempted to perform rituals on a hilltop during a storm. This probably sounds obvious, but you'd be amazed at some of the things I've seen people do in the name of magick. If there is a thunderstorm in your vicinity, then by all means perform this magick in a safe place, where you can see the lightning and hear the thunder. That makes the magick a lot more fun, but it is in no way essential, so don't seek it out. The real power of lightning comes from within.

We came across this concept when studying a particular form of Kabbalistic magick that mentioned lightning. We put it into practice and it worked. Since then we have noticed how often electricity is referred to in sacred texts and occult works.

When you look at the science behind lightning, it hints at the beautiful occult truth of electricity. Electrical flow is caused when electrical charge is out of balance. If there is a negative charge, a flow of electrons comes in to restore balance. This is what magick does; it creates a flow of change that brings balance to your life. This is a massive over-simplification, but it's worth reading about electricity because it is a symbolic echo of the way we can slip out of balance, and then attract a flow of change to restore balance.

It's also worth noting that when we see lightning strike the ground, the bright fork of lightning we see most clearly is actually the return stroke, as the energy travels back to the cloud. It isn't a bolt from above that we see, but the light returning to the heavens. This means there is an almost continual energy exchange going on. With a lightning strike happening somewhere in the world almost every second, we are always in contact with the heavens.

In this book, you will use the power of imagined lightning to contact angels and get them to work for you. Remember that electricity is a force that makes our brains and bodies function, and it is the same force that thunders and flashes from the heavens.

To use the power of lightning all you need to do is imagine a bolt of lightning striking you when you say an angel's name. Ideally, you should imagine a blue light thundering down from above, striking you and returning to the heavens.

When you come to the part of the book that describes the ritual in detail you will see the * symbol, and that shows when you need to imagine this lightning bolt. Most of the best magickal secrets are astonishingly simple, and they can sound so simple that you may dismiss them. You may be worried that your imagination is not clear enough. Do not worry about these things. Simply imagine a bolt of lightning striking you and connecting you to the angel you are naming.

If, for example, you are asked to call out to Raziel, you will say RAH-ZEE-ELL*, and as you call the name you picture lightning coming down from the clouds, striking you and returning to heaven. Imagine that it forges a connection between yourself and the angel.

We all imagine in different ways. Some people can picture things cinematically. Others hear sounds, and some people can only imagine conceptually. Whatever form of imagination you use, you can imagine something that will be effective.

Some people report feeling a tingle of electricity, others feel the full force of the energy, and some people feel nothing. I know some people who see flashes of light and others who hear thunder. For some the experience is extremely real, and for others it is a mundane part of the process. It doesn't matter what your experience of this technique feels like, so long as you actually perform the technique.

Do not overthink it or worry about whether you are getting it right. Imagine the lightning when you call the name, and that will forge a connection between you and the named angel without fail.

The Angel of Universal Secrets

The next secret is to make use of an easily-contacted angel, who makes the rest of the work simple. The angel in charge of this operation is the archangel Raziel. In this book you get access to all the tools required to contact Raziel, who then gives you access to the other angels in this book. Raziel is the gatekeeper of this magick.

To contact Raziel, you will first speak to an aspect of Raziel known as Arzel. In traditional magick, the angel Arzel is used to give you access to the powers of other angels. When you look at the original Hebrew, the spelling of Arzel is identical to the spelling of Raziel, apart from *one silent letter*. In other words, when said out loud, *they are the same name.* The Gallery of Magick believe that the angel Arzel is actually an aspect of Raziel. Arzel is the gateway angel to the archangel Raziel.

Many people report that Arzel is the easiest angel to call. You simply call for help (without any sigil or any ritual other than relaxation), and you feel a presence. The same is not true of the traditional Raziel, who can be difficult to contact. By calling first to Arzel, you are given access to Raziel, who grants you contact with any of the seventy-two angels.

As our investigations into this magick continued, we found an additional method for ensuring that Arzel hears your call. By reciting part of Psalm 80 of the Tehillim, you can call Arzel. All you need to do is face East and say:

Kosu hariym tzilah va'anafeha arzey-El

The actual translation of this verse is, 'The hills were covered with the shadow of it, and the boughs thereof were like the goodly cedars.' Although the transliteration of the Hebrew includes the phrase 'arzey-El', there is no direct mention of an angel called Arzel. Despite this, the call seems to work with dramatic efficiency, probably because angel names are frequently encoded in Biblical passages. Indeed, the names of the seventy-two angels are derived from this very style of three-letter encoding. Lines from the psalms are used to contact the angels, so it is little wonder that this psalm can also be used to call on Arzel, who then grants access to Raziel. (Interestingly, many people who call Arzel, catch a brief scent of cedars.)

We have also contacted Raziel directly, using full evocation, to check that our approach was correct. The answers we received made it clear to us that our method works. That is all we needed to know.

In terms of practical use, you will call on Arzel using the following pronunciations: ARE-ZELL, ARE-ZALE, and ARE-ZAY-ELL, followed by a direct call to Raziel. This method covers all the traditional pronunciations, and leads you to a sound that is very close to the pronunciation of Raziel, making contact with Raziel occur easily.

People will argue about magickal pronunciation for years – literally years, even decades – but there is no finer method for finding out what works best than experimentation. We have taken all this knowledge and the most detailed experiments have shown that this combination of pronunciations is the best approach. Do not worry about getting it exactly right. The angels will sense your call, and do not sit on high waiting for the correct pronunciation. When they hear your call, they respond.

When you call as instructed, know that you are calling Raziel, who will come to you easily, and brings a sense of light and peace that makes contact with other angels simple. Raziel is said to hold the secrets of the universe, and this gives you the power to contact angels and get them to perform alchemy in your life.

The opening phrase used in the ritual is:

NAH-KAH EE-AH-OH-EH

NAH-KAH is a simple way to pronounce the Hebrew word NawKar. (For those with an interest in Hebrew, this is spelt Nun Kaph Resh.) This word usually means 'recognized', but when stated in the active form it can mean 'to recognize'. So you are saying that you will recognize EE-AH-OH-EH. This is my preferred way of pronouncing the Tetragrammaton, the so-called unutterable name of God. As such, the phrase means that you intend to recognize God. This statement helps to get Raziel's attention and cooperation.

If you believe in God, there's no problem. If you don't, then as an occultist you probably believe in some force that creates and provides, and you know that all magick is an attempt to contact and guide this force. Know that when you make the above call, you are reaching out to the creative force of the universe, to recognize it in your life. When you say NAH-KAH EE-AH-OH-EH you are calling for magick to thunder through your life.

By making this call you urge Raziel to be much more co-operative, and the system works far, far more effectively. You may also find that your magick provides results that make you appreciate the wonder, dignity and grace of your life more deeply.

Singing to Angels

If you want an angel to hear your request, you should sing.

You've heard about choirs of angels? This is the language they speak. Your singing voice is always heard by an angel. This is one of my favorite occult discoveries.

We got the clue to this truth when going through all the different versions of *The Sixth and Seventh Book of Moses*. Most of the original source texts do not refer to angels at all. There is one text, however, that names various angels and also recommends calling them in a specific way, as well as blowing a horn. We didn't have a horn to experiment with, so we tried making a horn-like sound. The best we could do was to sing a note. It worked.

If you sing an angel's name, the results can be astonishing. You don't need to sing well, or even sing a particular tune. You don't need to sing loudly or impressively. All you need to do is make the angelic name sound as though it is being sung.

When you come to a name that requires singing, you will see this symbol *. This is the same symbol for picturing a lightning strike. So, when you see * after a name, know that the name should be sung, while picturing the lightning bolt.

If, for example, you are asked to say RAH-ZEE-ELL *, then you should picture the bolt of lightning while singing the name RAH-ZEE-ELL.

It can take some practice to get this right, because you are doing more than one thing at once, but do not worry about getting this perfectly right. Your intent is more important than perfection.

If you require privacy, and cannot sing out loud, then call the name in your mind, but imagine that it is being sung loudly, to the ends of the universe.

Preparing for Contact

The following Shem Talisman is used for making contact with the seventy-two angels.

In *Magickal Angels* and *The Greater Magickal Angels* I used two traditional talismans, which have always been effective. In 2015, after much thought, The Gallery of Magick decided that we would reveal some of our more closely guarded secrets. This talisman is one of those secrets. The content of the talisman is traditional, but our presentation of it in this form is unique. We have found this talisman to be the most effective for contacting the seventy-two angels.

You do not need to know what the Hebrew letters say, but as many people appear to be interested, I will offer a brief overview.

The three outer circles of text are lines from Exodus. The outer line is written from right to left, as is normal for Hebrew. The second line is written from left to right, with the next line again written from right to left. If you take any letter from the outer circle and scan toward the center of the talisman, the three letters you see spell the root of an angelic name.

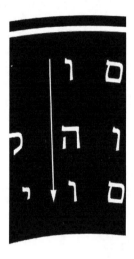

In the above example, the three letters are Vav, Heh and Vav, which are the root letters for the angelic name Vehuel. (Each name is created by adding 'el' or 'iah' to the end of the three-letter root.)

In the white circle, the outer ring is a series of divine names. The inner circle is the text of a psalm traditionally used to call Raziel, and this text is spoken during the ritual. The central triangle contains an encoding of the letters that form the name of God.

To create the above talisman for your own use, you have several options.

If you have the paperback, you can photocopy the talisman, cut it out and you are ready to go. You can even use the talisman in the book, and then when contact with Raziel is established, you turn to the page with the angelic sigil. (You do not need to keep the talisman in sight throughout the ritual.)

If you have the e-book, then you can print out the talisman by downloading it from the website

http://galleryofmagick.com/angelic-templates/

Some people have taken photographs of the page in the e-book, but it's better to download the image from the website.

Talismans and sigils work whether or not you 'charge' them psychically, but many people find they get better results if they activate the images with magickal energy. What follows is a technique that can be used to charge the Shem Talisman, as well as the angelic sigils.

The following technique even works on electronic versions of the talisman and the sigils. So long as you see a sigil while it is being charged, it will remain charged, even when used on a different device at a later date. So you could charge the sigil in the print book, and then use the sigil in the e-book and you will get results. Or you could charge the sigil on your laptop, and it will work on an iPad. This is because when you charge a sigil you are actually taking it within yourself, and binding yourself to the angelic energy.

This technique is fairly simple, although it does require some use of your imagination. Do not worry if you are unable to visualize clearly. We all have different qualities of imagination, and however you imagine is right for you, so it will work.

Charge the Shem Talisman first, and then you can charge each sigil when you know you will be using it at some point in the future. You can perform this charging ritual just moments before you perform the main ritual, or months in advance, and the effect will remain as strong.

Whether you are charging a sigil or the Shem Talisman the process is the same, although to make the following description simpler, I will refer only to the charging of the talisman in this chapter.

Find a quiet place where you can relax and get comfortable, without being disturbed. Let your eyes pass over the talisman, scanning over the shapes of the letters and the lines that makes up the image. Look at the letters as though they are merely shapes. Do not try to read them or understand them.

After doing this for a few moments, take a breath and imagine the sun, and feel its mighty power. Imagine the sun shrinking down and as it shrinks it moves towards your chest. It settles in your heart as a tiny, brilliant star. Remain aware of this brilliant star within you, and gaze at the talisman. Now imagine that the sky above you is filled with powerful storm clouds, ready to strike lightning. Look at the talisman again and imagine that the image of the talisman moves into your heart. You can actually imagine the talisman rising from the book and moving into your heart. If you find it difficult to picture this, simply *know* that the talisman is moving within you. When you feel that the talisman has reached your heart, imagine a bolt of lightning descending from the heavens and striking the talisman in your heart. You may feel a pleasant physical sensation as the talisman ignites. You may feel nothing. Whatever you feel, the work is done and the image has been empowered within you.

Let your gaze pass over the talisman once more. Simply look at it, but as you do, know that your eyes are tracing over lines and shapes that are now contained within your heart. You are already connected to the angels before you even attempt to make contact.

Although this ritual can take as long as five minutes, it can be over in seconds, and that is fine.

The most important aspect of this ritual is that you perform it with serious commitment, but then you should not worry about whether you did it well enough or whether it worked. By performing this ritual, and inviting the sigil or talisman into your heart, you made it work. Nobody else is judging its effectiveness, so there is no need to worry about whether the angels will think you've done a good enough job. This is personal magick, and you have chosen to connect yourself to the image, and that is all that matters.

Choosing an Angel

Later in the book all seventy-two angels are listed, along with their powers, all the details you need for making contact, and the angel's sigil. The listed powers may not be the traditional powers that you see in some books, or on the internet, but working from primary sources, and working with these angels directly for several decades, we have found these to be their main powers.

You must decide which angel suits your task. In some cases, you may want to use two or more angels at once. Avoid using more than one angel unless you *really* feel you need to do so. One perfectly chosen angel will often do a better job than three that *might* help the situation.

If you do use more than one angel on a single problem, you should perform the ritual with your request for one angel, finish it, and then repeat the entire process for the next angel, later on the same day. This is quite time consuming, but works better than cramming several sigils onto your table and making a mass of requests to several angels at once.

If you can, choose one angel that best suits your needs.

Sometimes, it will take a little thought to work out how an angel's power applies to you. If an angel is said to have the power to Destroy Enemies, it's fairly clear when you would use that angel. If you have an enemy, you can choose to destroy them. There is a lot of freedom in how you interpret this, though. You could choose to destroy your enemy's ability to harm you, their ability to work effectively, or you could destroy their personal life or health. The angels can do any of this, so remember that for every description, there is a wide interpretation. You are the one who chooses how the angel's power will be used.

There is no karmic backlash. If you earn great wealth, you will not be punished with poverty. If you stop an enemy from ruining your life, you will not be burned at a later date. Your Magick is about making choices, and impressing those choices on reality, rather than being subject to the whims of chaos or the decisions of those who would exploit or harm you.

Also be aware that some of the more obscure-sounding powers are actually some of the most useful. When scanning through the book to see which powers you want to use, it's tempting to go straight to Poiel for fame, wealth and to have all your desires met. If you are planning wisely, though, you might first want to Learn About Desires Through Dreams. This doesn't sound half as impressive as instant wealth, but one of the most difficult jobs we have in magick is choosing exactly what we want. Often, we think we know what we want, perform the magick, get what we asked for and regret it greatly. I could fill a book with such stories. So learning about your desires through dreams has its value.

As you read through the book, be wary of leaping for the quick fixes, and know there is enormous benefit to be obtained from all these powers.

The only way to choose an angel is to read about the powers of all the angels, become familiar with what they can do, and know exactly what it is that you want to change.

When you read about the angel, you will get an intuitive feeling for what it can achieve. The basic descriptions I give are a starting point, and all angels have additional powers, which may be revealed to you as you work with them. So have the confidence to choose an angel. This urges you to really analyze your problem in the first place, and sometimes that can be half the battle.

Once you have chosen your angel, learn how to pronounce the name and the relevant invocation chant, and study the sigil for a few minutes. You may also want to empower the sigil at this point, as described earlier, so that everything is ready when you come to the ritual itself.

Crafting Your Request

For each angel you will find a descriptive outline of the powers and skills of that particular angel, but I have not written down the request you should make to the angel, because it is far more powerful to write you own request and then read it out during the ritual.

You may feel that talking directly to the angel - without anything written down - is more appealing, and that *can* work. When you are starting out, however, I suggest writing down something that is clear, precise and not too long. You do not need to spend fifteen minutes explaining to the angel why you want some extra money. You only need to ask.

When I describe the Master Ritual later in this book, I use the example of a struggling writer who wants more success. As such, he has chosen Poiel (pronounced PAW-EE-ELL), because two of Poiel's powers are described as **To Increase Fame and Fortune** and **To Bring Fame Through Talent**. Those are ideal for a struggling writer who truly believes his talent deserves to be recognized, and who is in need of some unexpected money and ongoing wealth to give him the time to write.

Step 1: Opening the call

Your call should always begin with: 'I call on thee, powerful PAW-EE-ELL (or whichever angel you are calling), who has power to…', and then you add the angel's powers *as you see them*.

Based on what you have read in this book, and what you are seeking, come up with a phrase that sums up the angel's powers. Again, don't worry about getting this right. Perfection is not required. By naming the powers, you are asking the angel to *use* these powers.

In this example, the struggling writer might say, 'I call on thee, powerful PAW-EE-ELL, who has power to bring fame, success and fortune that is asked for.'

You could just as easily write, 'I call on thee, powerful PAW-EE-ELL, who has power to help writers.' You could even say, 'I call on thee, powerful PAW-EE-ELL, who has power to bring me fame through my talents.'

I could have included samples for every angel, but it does not work as well that way. It works best when you write your own.

Step 2: The Summary

After this opening call you should summarize what it is that you want, stating, 'It is my will…' and then summarizing your desire in a short sentence.

Here, and ideal statement would be, 'It is my will to become a wealthy and successful writer.'

Do not write, 'It is my will to become a wealthy writer by publishing my first novel, *Adventures in Timber Town*, through Deep Harbor Publishing.' Although there are times when you want to target your magick as directly as this, for a general request for increased success in an area, leave room for general success.

There will be more on this subject later, but be careful of limiting your magick by being too specific. If, of course, the whole aim of your ritual is to obtain an exceptionally specific result, such as, 'It is my will to sign with the literary agent Morvine Barnes,' then say exactly that. But when you are seeking general success in an area, phrase it so that you give the angel room to surprise you. When you leave the magick open, angels have more ways to bring you the results you want. Unexpected results that give you what you want are often the best results.

Step 3: Sending Out Feelings

You now write, 'I ask that you go forth and…' Here you state what you want in a little more detail, and instead of focusing on how you want the result to manifest, you focus on how the manifestation will *make you feel*.

In this example you might say, 'I ask that you go forth and bring me money in the form of good fortune, that will give me the wealth I need to write freely and happily. I ask that you go forth and make all my books sell extremely well, bringing me wealth and success.'

Whatever you write should create a positive emotional reaction in you, and a sense of how exciting that result would be.

Step 4: The Moment of Alchemy

Once you have stated your desire, you should make a statement about the change that you want to occur. Magick is a process of alchemy, where you and your circumstances change.

Rather than focusing purely on the positive, magick works best when you focus on the discomfort you feel at the outset, and then imagine how those feelings will change when the magick works.

You are not pleading with the angel or trying to justify your actions. You are showing where you have been and where you are going, and how the magick will benefit you.

Do not try to sound worthy. Concentrate on honestly explaining your feelings, with brief, clear sentences.

In this example, our struggling writer might now say, 'I have suffered for years without being able to write. I have felt great pain in my current employment. I ask for enough money to come to me that I can become a fulltime writer and live out the gift I was born with. I ask for this transformation, and I feel the change you can bring, as I become a wealthy and successful writer.'

Note how this states the past problem, and acknowledges what it will feel like to have the transformation take place. When you actually say the words during the ritual you should remember your pain or discomfort or anger at the current situation, and as you continue talking, feel the relief that the magick will bring. This moment of emotional alchemy is absolutely essential for the success of the ritual.

Step 5: The Promise

In the next section you need to show that you will be involved with the magick, and that you are offering to contribute to the process. This will vary depending on what you are asking.

If you are asking for protection from an enemy, there may not be much you can do other than remain as confident and calm as possible. That will do. In most cases, however, you will get a general sense of what you can do to help the situation. Again, don't be too specific here. Our writer should not make a list of promises about what novels he plans to complete, or suggest any timeline. Instead, something like this would work. 'I will do my work as a writer, and I let go of all hope and confusion, for I know that you can bring me what I need.'

Notice that as well as offering to get involved, this statement also shows the intention to believe in the magick. Make this promise even if you have doubts about the magick. The intention to let go of fear, doubt, confusion and even hope, while knowing that the angel *will* help, can lead to you opening up to magickal results.

Step 6: Closing Your Request

The final part of your request should always be the same. 'I seal this command with the word of power: AH-RAH-REE-TAH. As you angels have come in peace, go in peace. It is done.'

Writing a good, clear request, using these steps, will lead to effective magick. Once again, don't overthink this and spend weeks crafting the perfect request. Angels listen if you say nothing more than, 'Help me out of my misery'. But if you want the best and most direct results, then wording your request as described is the best approach.

Targeting Your Magick

Often you want general results, but sometimes you want extremely specific results. Rather than requesting peace in your neighborhood, you may want a specific neighbor to shut up or move away. Instead of hoping for more success in your music career, you might want to book a gig at a particular venue. If you work in sales or the markets, you might want results that are directed at those income streams.

Most of the time, when people write to me, it is because they are looking for specific results, and this is why the books I write are often aimed at specific areas, such as bringing in quick money, building wealth or finding romantic partners. How does this relate to angels?

Although I always recommend trying a general approach where possible – because it leaves more room for the spirits to do their work with more imagination than you could dream of – the fabulous thing about angels is that you can be extremely specific. The danger here is that if you are too specific you may reduce your chances of getting a result.

You need to develop the skill of knowing when to be specific and when to be general. If you want more money, then do general wealth workings. If you want to get a particular product you're selling to be more popular, then you can do a ritual for that product.

An approach that many of us use is to do a general working, and then follow it up with a specific working. Some years ago I was living in a relatively pleasant area, but the immediate neighborhood changed and there were terrible fights all around, inside houses and sometimes in the street. The whole area began to feel aggressive. I knew that if I tried a specific working to get the most troublesome family to leave, I would have limited results, because there was still so much fiery energy in the street. First I did a working to bring general calm to the area, and then I did a working to make the family quieter and calmer. Finally, I did a working to get them to leave. That was a lot of work and quite a bit of magickal effort on my part, but compared to the endless hours of screaming and fighting, it was worthwhile.

Only you can judge what will work for you. If you try something specific and don't get the result you want within a few weeks, you might want to try something more general, and then move to the specific.

If there's a really strong sense of urgency, however, then go straight for the specific. If you're being attacked by a cruel enemy, then perform magick to subdue and silence that enemy until you can plan your next move.

Angelic magick requires a flexible approach. General workings are extremely powerful and will continue to affect your life for months to come, but when you want to direct your magick to something more specific, you can.

I will repeat the warning. Do not go for the specific unless it's required. In the example of our struggling writer, I suggested an open approach, because there are so many pathways to success. If he had pushed one novel to one publisher, his chances of success would be limited, and failure would remain more likely than success. By seeking more income to write, and more success as a writer in general, he was giving the magick a chance to work in hundreds of unexpected ways. Often, that is exactly what you want.

Feeding the Angels

Many people feel that they should offer the angels something for their work, such as incense, candles or prayers. In my experience this is not required, and merely wastes time and makes a mess, but one thing angels do appreciate is when you share the benefits of your magick. This is not essential every time, but when you can share magickal results, it is a good habit to get into.

When you perform a ritual for yourself, and give some of the energy or result away, your own results will be improved. This is not an essential part of the process, and it doesn't work for everything. If you are seeking the love of a particular partner, for example, that's not really energy you want to share around. If you want to protect your home or earn more money, however, you can certainly share that.

I've never been a big fan of tithing. Giving away ten percent of your income without thinking about it or feeling it is like taxing yourself all over again, for no good reason. If you *like* giving, you should *enjoy* the act of giving as an experience. I've met many people who tithe, but think it would be wrong to tithe with the intention of making more money, so when they give they try to pretend it's purely for the good of the other person. That seems like self-deception at best, and also a wasted opportunity.

Giving works best when you actually enjoy it, and when you revel in the knowledge that giving will bring *you* more as well. This is true whether you're giving away cash, gifts or magickal results and energy.

There are two main reasons that giving is good. The obvious reason is that it helps others, and as you become more powerful that just seems like the right thing to do. We'll not talk about karma, but let's just say it's wise to share the love.

Another reason, and the more 'selfish' reason, is that when you get good at giving, you get better at receiving. This is what all the new age and self-help books tell you. What they don't tell you is that you can give magickal power instead of money, and this works best when you are using spirits such as angels.

How does this work in practice? When you are writing your request, before you come to Step 6, all you need to do is write something along the lines of, 'Share the benefits of this magick with...' You can then name a specific person, the people in your street or anybody else you like. You can even offer the magickal result to 'those who need it most.'

If you like you can get specific with percentages, or even give half away. You can talk to the angel in detail, at this point. Often I will say, 'Please share ten percent of this magickal result with my loved ones'. Most importantly, feel pleasure in the act of giving out of pure generosity, but also feel pleasure in knowing this can bring more to you.

This approach flies in the face of most New Age books, which suggest that giving should be selfless. They clearly haven't tried the above method.

You can pass the result on to somebody you love, somebody you loathe or pick a stranger. The act of sharing your magick in this way can make it more enjoyable and often makes it more effective. Don't feel obliged to use this technique every time. If the magickal result feels like an energy that should be kept to yourself, then keep it to yourself. The angels do not judge.

What if you simply want to help another person by using magick, without gaining any results for yourself? Many occultists advise against doing magick for others without their knowledge, because you may be interfering with their true will, but every interaction we have with another human could be seen as interference. Angel magick can easily be directed at others. If you feel the urge to help somebody in the real world, feel free to perform magick for them, but you might want to keep the magickal act secret even when the result manifests.

Pronunciation

The rituals in this book contain many names, sounds and phrases that will not be familiar to you. Everything can be pronounced in several ways, depending on how you interpret the original language, your native language, age, education and your local accent. I have included a phonetic pronunciation beneath the words in BOLD CAPITALS. This is the pronunciation that will work.

This book is absolutely Pronunciation Proof. The important letters and words are already included in the Shem Talisman and each angelic sigil, so even if you pronounce everything incorrectly, it will work.

However, the pronunciation is quite simple. For the most part, you just say the words in capitals as though they are English. (The pronunciation contained in this book is not always conventional or truly authentic, but has been carefully researched and tested to get results. You can trust that it will work, whatever your accent or style of speaking.)

So where it says *Kosu hariym tzilah va'anafeha arzey-El* you will see the words KOH-SUE HAH-REE-EEM TZIL-AH VAH-ANNA-FEHA ARE-ZELL in capitals. The capitalized words are a pronunciation guide, showing you exactly how to say the words.

KOH sounds like the word *oh* with a *k* in front of it.

SUE is the same as the word *sue*.

HAH is like *ah* with *h* at the front.

EEM is like *seem* without the *s*.

And so on. As you can see, it's quite easy to get these sounds right. Mostly, this is just like reading English, but to ensure you find this easy, I will now look at some of the most common sounds.

AH

The **AH** sound is used throughout the book, so it's worth noting that this sounds like the *ah* sound you get in *ma* and *pa*. Simply say *ma* without the *m* and you've got the right sound.

EH

EH is like the middle part of the word *set*. Say *set* without the *s* or the *t* and you've got **EH**.

UH

UH is *up* without the *p*. So if you see the sound **PUH**, you know that sounds like *put* without the *t*.

AW

AW is like *awe*, or like *raw* without the *r*. So if you see **BAW**, you know it sounds like the word *awe* with **b** at the front.

AY

AY is like *pay* without the *p*. So if you see **NAY**, it's like *pay* with *n* instead of *p*.

TZ

TZ sounds like the end of *cats*. In context, it sounds a bit more like **TZ** than **TS**. So when you say **TZIL-AH**, when you make the *ts* sound, it comes out as **TZIL-AH**.

CH

Authentic Hebrew often uses the *ch* sound that you hear in the Scottish word *loch*, or the German *achtung*. You can study YouTube videos of native speakers using these words, to learn the *ch* sound. Alternatively, you can simply make a *k* sound when you see **CH**.

To illustrate this, you will often see the word **CHAH**. This is the *ch* sound described above, followed by *ah*. If you can't make the guttural *ch* sound, then replace it with a *k*. **CHAH** becomes **KAH**, and sounds like *ah* with a *k* at the front.

If this sounds complicated, remember that for the most part, you're just reading English sounds. The only real difference is **CH**. You can be bold and try for the correct sounding **CH**, or just sound it as **K** instead. The book is Pronunciation Proof and what you say will work.

If you really don't like reading the Hebrew, there is an alternative. For each invocation chant, I list the appropriate Psalm. For Yeliel, for example, it is Psalm 22:19. That means you look for Psalm 22, line 19. In the King James Bible, that reads as, 'But be not thou far from me, O Lord: O my strength, haste thee to help me.' If you struggle with the Hebrew, simply use the correct English psalm in its place. You will still need to learn the angelic names, but that shouldn't be too difficult.

Remember that the line from the psalm does not name the angel directly, or even relate to the angel's powers. The angel's name is encoded in the text of the psalm, and that is all that matters.

About one percent of readers have asked for audio recordings to make it clear what the words should sound like, but I do not feel that these would help. The way a New York woman pronounces these words would be different to the way a man from London would say them. We have provided English approximations of the words that have worked for people we know all over the world. They work, and most importantly, you should remember that the sigils make the book Pronunciation Proof. The words, names and phrases appear visually in the book, so even if you get the pronunciation wrong, it doesn't matter – you have absorbed the words visually, and this will enable you to make angelic contact. I am making this point repeatedly because I know that people worry about pronunciation more than any other aspect of magick.

These invocations are an important part of the process, because each contains a letter encoding of the angel's name. This is why the angel responds to the call. (Other psalms can also be used effectively, and there are many suggested alternatives, but you can't go wrong with the psalms included in this book.)

Whether you choose Hebrew or English, let the words vibrate from the base of your lungs, rising through your throat and out of your mouth as though you are speaking them to the horizon. Ideally, they should not be whispered, but allowed to resonate in your throat as they pass out of you, especially when the words are sung. You don't need to sing the whole ritual, but if you feel the urge to, there's no reason why you can't.

Letting the words vibrate may not always be possible, as mentioned earlier, if you require privacy. If you cannot say the words out loud, whispering is better than nothing. If you must perform the work in silence, you can say the words in your head. If you do whisper or perform the work silently, make it feel as though you are calling to the ends of the universe.

Using The Sigil

This is an example of a sigil:

The artwork in the exact center is the angelic seal for the specific angel you are calling. In this sigil, it looks like this:

If you are viewing this in color, you will see that the angelic seal in the center is colored red. If you are using the printed book you have a couple of options. One is to know that the angelic seal in the center can be *thought of* as red. You can imagine it as red and that is good enough. Another option is to photocopy the image, and then trace over the central seal with a red marker pen.

Do not worry that the magick will fail if you don't use red. When we first developed this sigil we didn't use colors for over a decade. This is a refinement that can help, but it's an optional extra rather than an essential part of the working. During the ritual you should look at this sigil just before calling the angel's name. In particular, look at the angel's seal at the very center. You do not need to stare or focus too hard. Simply be aware of the shape and that will help establish contact.

The rest of the symbol is made up of divine words of power and phrases that protect you and make the magick effective. The angel's name is written in Hebrew, and in an angelic script. The invocation chant is written in the black ring. The lines of the square contain the call to Arzel.

As part of the ritual you will be told to scan your eyes over parts of the sigil. During the first scan you pass your eyes over the letters in the square part of the sigil, to connect to Arzel. You are not trying to read or understand the words. This is a quiet moment where you let the words sink into your soul. Scan the uppermost line of the square, from right to left, as shown in the following diagram:

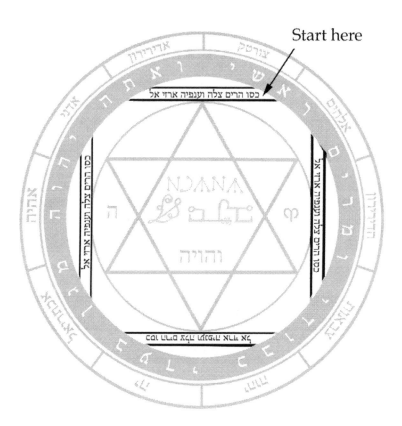

Now move to the line on the left, and scan your eyes from top to bottom. Move your eyes to the lowest line of the square and scan from left to right (even though the letters are upside down). Finally, scan your eyes over the right hand side of the square, from bottom to top.

Later in the ritual, you will scan the white letters in the black circle, because this is the Invocation Chant. Start at the top of the circle and scan anti-clockwise. Take the time to look at the shape of each letter. Some of the letters are upside down, but that's fine – just take in their shape with your eyes. You can scan the circle two times if you want, but there is no need to do any more than this.

This image shows you where to start your scan for the Invocation Chant. You always begin just to the left of the vertical line at the top of the circle. Scan your eyes anti-clockwise. Remember, you are not reading, but letting the shapes sink into your soul.

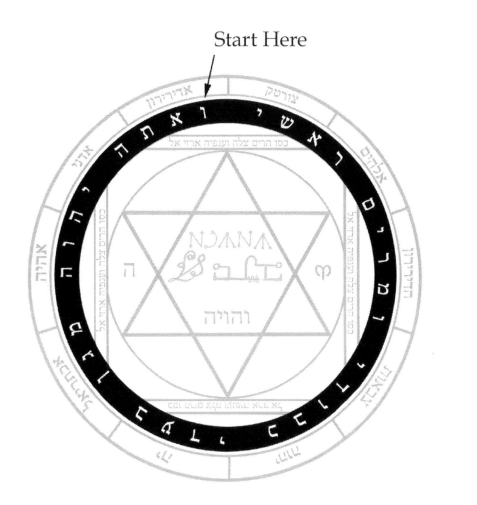

You can practice this now, using any sigil, so that you will be familiar with the process when you come to perform a ritual.

Eleven Days of Angelic Contact

Begin your working on a Thursday and continue the working for eleven days, so that the last time you perform the ritual is on a Sunday.

If you miss a day, due to unforeseen circumstances, do not try to catch up, but simply continue as before and finish on a Sunday. If you miss a day because you were lazy or lost interest, start again on the following Thursday, refining the ritual if need be.

Any time of day is fine, although some people say the hour before sunrise is best.

Contact is made from the moment you begin, and results may come about within minutes, hours or days, but continue the working for the full eleven days even when the result shows early.

If you absolutely can't start a working on a Thursday, start on a Monday. If you can't finish the ritual on a Sunday, keep going until you can finish on a Thursday. If you can't do any of these, just try to work the ritual as often as possible (but no more than once a day) until you get results, but be aware that eleven consecutive days, starting on a Thursday, is the best way to get results.

The Master Ritual

This chapter explains the Master Ritual used to contact and communicate with angels. In this example we will use the angel Poiel, being called to help a writer be more successful. You will see that there are various instructions, and certain things you have to say and do.

When you perform the ritual for yourself, ensure that you fully understand the instructions explained in the **Crafting Your Request** chapter, or results will be limited.

This example is used to familiarize you with the ritual, but these instructions and wordings are simplified and listed clearly in **Appendix A: The Master Ritual Simplified**, so you can easily construct rituals yourself.

Note that each time you see this symbol *, this is a moment where you perform the magickal lightning strike described in the earlier chapter, as well as singing the angelic name.

Find a time and place where you will not be disturbed.

Stand, facing East, with a small table or other surface before you, so you can see your talisman and sigil clearly when required. (You can sit or kneel on the floor if that is easier.)

Place the Shem Talisman before you.

Say:

This is the beginning. I open the way.

Reach both arms forward, holding them straight out in front of you, with the backs of the hands touching (thumbs toward the ground). Now move your hands apart, as though your palms are opening the space before you.

Gaze at the Shem Talisman gently for a few moments, and know that it will connect you to the seventy-two angels. Keep your eyes on the central triangle as you say:

I call on the inner world to know that this is my will.

NAH-KAH EE-AH-OH-EH
NAH-KAH EE-AH-OH-EH
NAH-KAH EE-AH-OH-EH

The talisman can stay within sight, but you do not need to keep looking at it now.

Picture the following images as clearly as you can, as you say:

I pass through the arch of stone.

> I walk through a field of golden corn.
> I am warmed by fire of the sun.
> I am cooled by water of the ocean.
> I am steady on the firm earth.
> I breathe a sweet breeze.
> I feel the weight of the earth beneath me.

Ask these questions of yourself, out loud, but do not attempt to answer them in any way:

> I ask, how did I come to be at peace?
> I ask, how did I let go of fear?
> I ask, how did I learn to manifest my dreams?

Imagine an orange glow on your left. Imagine a purple glow on your right. Imagine these lights for just a few moments.

Make sure the angelic sigil is before you. If you need to flip to a new page in the book, that's OK, you no longer need to see the Shem Talisman.

Gaze at the entire sigil, taking in its patterns, letters and shapes.

Scan your eyes over the letters in the square of your chosen sigil, as discussed earlier.

Say:

> I call on thee, Arzel (ARE-ZELL)* in the East,
> to connect me to the secret angels of the universe.
>
> Kosu hariym tzilah va'anafeha arzey-El
> (KOH-SUE HAH-REE-EEM TZIL-AH VAH-ANNA-FEHA ARE-ZELL)
>
> ARE-ZELL*, ARE-ZELL*, ARE-ZELL*
>
> ARZ-ALE*, ARZ-ALE*, ARZ-ALE*
>
> ARE-ZAY-ELL*, ARE-ZAY-ELL*, ARE-ZAY-ELL*
>
> I call on thee, Raziel (RAH-ZEE-ELL*) in the East
> to make me heard by the secret angels of the universe.
>
> RAH-ZEE-ELL*, RAH-ZEE-ELL*, RAH-ZEE-ELL*

VAH-HAH-DEH-REH-CHAH
TZ-LAH
REH-CHAB
AL-DEH-BAR-EH-MET
VAY-AHN-VAH-TZAY-DECK
VAY-TORE-AY-CHAR
NAW-RAH-AUGHT
YEH-ME-NAY-CHAH

Oh Raziel (RAH-ZEE-ELL*),
let my voice be heard by the
great angel Poiel (PAW-EE-ELL *)
I seal this command with the
word of power
AH-RAH-REE-TAH

Visually scan the letters of the Invocation Chant in the black circle, in an anti-clockwise direction.

Speak The Invocation Chant:

KEY RAW-TSAY EE-AH-OH-EH
BEH-AH-MAW YEH-FAH-AIR
AH-NAH-VEEM BEE-SHOO-AH

Glance at the sigil and Sing the Angel's name three times:

PAW-EE-ELL *, PAW-EE-ELL *, PAW-EE-ELL *

Speak Your Request to The Angel:

I call on thee, powerful PAW-EE-ELL *, who has power
to bring fame, success and fortune that is asked for.

It is my will to become a wealthy and successful writer.

I ask that you go forth and bring me money
in the form of good fortune, that will give
me the wealth I need to write freely and happily.
I ask that you go forth and make all
my books sell extremely well,

bringing me wealth and success.

I have suffered for years without being able to write.
I have felt great pain in my current employment.
I ask for enough money to come to me that
I can become a fulltime writer
and live out the gift I was born with.
I ask for this transformation,
and I feel the change you can bring,
as I become a wealthy and successful writer.

I will do my work as a writer,
and I let go of all hope and confusion,
for I know that you can bring me what I need.

I seal this command with the word of power:
AH-RAH-REE-TAH
As you angels have come in peace, go in peace. It is done.

What is the Experience of Contact Like?

For some people, the experience of angelic contact is nothing more than a ritualistic activity performed to get results. For others, a sense of direct contact with the angel occurs. In more developed relationships you can communicate directly with the angel and hear responses. If you are seeking results, then the form of contact you make is irrelevant, because the angel has heard and you will get your results.

You can, however, seek more direct contact with the angel, if you want to hear the angel speak, sense its presence or even glimpse a moment of its reality.

It's important to note that you do *not* need to sense the angel's presence. I've heard people worry about angelic magick, because they didn't see a huge, glowing, winged being appear before them. There is no need to worry, because sensing the angel is secondary to getting results. This chapter is included for two reasons. Firstly, it is something that many people have requested. Secondly, the magickal practice explained here is a good way to start evoking angels if that's something you're interested in doing.

When you perform the rituals as outlined, your experience is your own, so don't be worried about what happens. Some people sense peace, others sense power. You may feel cold enter the room, or even a wave of heat. Many people see small flashes of light, or catch a glimpse of the angel. For lots of people there is simply a tingle down the spine as you sense the angel close by. For a lot of people, though, there is no sensation at all, and that is fine. If you want to develop your connection to the angels into a more direct contact, then there are several things you can do.

Make sure that you use all your imaginative faculties when performing the ritual. When you say the words, 'I pass through the arch of stone. I walk through a field of golden corn,' and so on, imagine this with all your senses. Picture a stone archway of any kind in any location, but imagine how it looks, feel the sun or cold wind on your skin, smell the surrounding grass, water or earth, and let your hands brush the stone as you pass. When you move through the corn, hear it rustle, smell the air, see the shimmering corn. If you don't have a powerful imagination, keep working at this and it will improve.

When you ask the questions that begin with, 'I ask, how did I come to be at peace?', leave your mind blank. You are asking these questions to the void, as though they reflect truths about yourself, and you should seek no answer.

Most importantly, when you call an angel's name, do this with the feeling that you are actually calling to a real entity that exists and can hear you. This may sound obvious, but many people perform the rituals and make the calls into the room, or to themselves, rather than directly *to* the angel.

To get an idea of what I mean, sit in a room by yourself and say the words, 'Stop doing that.' It's meaningless, and doesn't have much impact. Now imagine there's somebody on the other side of the room, breaking something precious of yours. Say it again. You'll notice there's not only a difference in your voice, but even though you are pretending, it feels as though you are saying it *to* somebody. This is how you contact angels. You imagine they are there. You don't need to picture them, but you need to imagine that they *are* there, and that you are actually talking to them rather than simply saying their names.

If you call the name of a friend, you expect your friend to pay attention. It's the same with an angel. When you call that name, know you are heard.

You must now follow this up by leaving space for the angel to respond. If you simply call out and then continue with the ritual, or end the ritual, there isn't much chance for the angel to respond. It's like calling out to your friend and before you get an answer you start talking again.

You can do this when you call the angel's name three times. At that point, wait in silence for a few moments, or minutes, allowing yourself to sense the angel. Do not force yourself to imagine, do not try to see the angel. All you need do is remain quiet and know that the angel you have called is present. Imagine that you are sitting quietly with a friend, and nothing needs to be said. Remain aware of the angel's presence. If the angel wants to make itself known, seen or heard, it will happen. Do not strive for this. Leave room for it, and let whatever happens happen. If you feel nothing, know you have been heard by the angel anyway, and continue with the ritual.

If you want to communicate with angels directly, rather than during another ritual, you can ask the angel for direct communication. This works best when you have already achieved a magickal result from the angel. By doing some work together, that manifests in reality, you have connected with the angel in a way that is extremely powerful.

Once you have obtained a result, you simply change your request, making the statement that you want to communicate with the angel, sense its presence and work with it in an ongoing way. You do not need to pray, beg, plead or promise anything for this contact to take place. Simply perform an eleven-day ritual, asking the angel to make contact. During those eleven days you may see signs – such as feathers, or angelic names. You may feel direct and immediate contact. Many people say they hear a rush of air, or feel like a wing has passed over them. Others feel warmth and light. You might only feel the slightest sense of another consciousness. Ultimately, this sense of consciousness is what you're looking for. You are not communicating with a puppet or drawing or imagined being – you should remember that angels are conscious beings with distinctive personalities and voices.

After asking to make contact with the angel, you can then gaze at the angel's sigil at any time that you want to make contact. Sing the angel's name three times, and allow the angel to make itself known. Leave some space for the angel. Wait a while in silence.

Do not strive too hard to make contact. I often think back to a time when I was trying to obtain lucid dreams, and I purchased a dream machine that would monitor my eye movements, and flash lights in my eyes while I slept. It was meant to trigger lucid dreams. I slept with that thing strapped around my head for months, and nothing happened. When I finally gave up and swore I'd never use it again, I had a beautiful, crystal clear lucid dream. I had given up, and the result I wanted came about. It is the same with angelic contact. If you strive, you can push results away. If you know that the contact *has* already been made the moment you look at the sigil and sing the angel's name, then you merely have to wait for the conversation to start.

Once you establish this sort of relationship with an angel, where it will appear when called directly, you can ask for guidance regarding its powers and how it can help you. You may hear a voice, get a sense of understanding or even see the angel before you. Every experience is different, and if you only get a hint of an angel's presence, do not be disappointed. Equally, if you see an angel standing before you, do not be afraid.

Making direct contact with angels is a hit and miss affair, and results depend on your state of mind, your needs, the magickal work you've done and many other factors. You may find that contact comes easily and often, or is an occasional gift. When you do make contact though, even for a moment, you will know that it is worthwhile.

If you work with these methods, you should gain some sense of an angel's presence, and more gifted people will be able to communicate directly with angels. Remember, though, that you can get results even if it feels like there's nothing listening and no magick happening. So long as you act as though the magick is real, it will work for you.

After the Ritual

When you perform magick one of the most difficult things to do is 'let go', and yet most people agree that if you long for results, they evade you. The best magick usually happens when you perform a ritual and genuinely forget about it.

In most magick books, especially those for beginners, you are told that if you Lust For Result, you cancel out your magick. That isn't always the case, but it happens so often that learning to overcome this eagerness for a result is important.

Letting go helps because you get out of the way of the magick. It's as though you're handing it over to somebody else to deal with, and trusting that they can do the job. Imagine asking somebody to drive you to the airport, and then giving them directions the whole way, when you don't even know the way. You'd annoy the driver and probably get lost. It's best if you sit back and let them take you to the airport. Let go, trust you'll get there and you will. It doesn't matter how.

I once helped instruct an actor with magick, to assist with finding an agent in a new country. Tired of being shunned in his own country, he'd planned a move to the US. He sent out his CV and showreel to a bunch of agents and performed the magick we'd discussed. He expected to be ignored, because he'd been ignored for two years in his own country. It wasn't that he doubted the magick. He just thought it would take a few months for people to pay him any attention, so he forgot about it all and got on with his life. The next morning, four agents asked to meet him.

If he'd been sitting there all night, wondering how well it was going, who would reply, and what they thought of him, it would not have worked so well.

If you can find a way to let go, that's ideal. Having absolute trust in your magick is one way. But many people find it difficult to let go, because when you do magick you are, after all, trying to change things in your world. You're doing magick because you really want something.

It is perfectly fine to desire your result, even though many occultists would say you should let go of all desire. If you find yourself thinking about the result you're aiming for, you shouldn't panic and worry that your Lust For Result is ruining your work. Instead, simply imagine that the end result has *already* come about and feels good. Don't try to work out how it came about, just imagine that it did. Take a moment to do this and your Lust For Result will fade.

This is such a simple technique that it's easy to dismiss, but it's very powerful. It's far better to use this small trick, than to put a lot of energy into avoiding thinking about the result you want.

Also, it's important to open the pathways. That is, if you're doing money magick, you should be out there doing something that can bring in money. Seek opportunities. Don't just sit and wait for cash to arrive. Cash does arrive out of the blue, sometimes, but if you want it on a regular basis, you must open the pathways for the magick to work by actually pushing your life forward.

You will constantly be thinking about your magickal results. You have to. You can't do magick to further your career and then forget about your career.

It's OK to really, really desire your result, so long as you don't dwell on the magick itself, and your eager need for a result. If you find yourself worrying, dwelling, hoping or – worst of all – wondering *how* the magick will manifest, then you need to occupy your mind. Imagine the end result, feel good about it, as though it's already happened. Then get on with something else.

This way, you can keep thinking about your magick, keep working towards you results, and Lust For Result is no longer a danger.

It does help, however, if you open yourself to feelings of enjoyment and gratitude in the present moment. When you are enjoying, you are not wanting, and so you open yourself to receiving. The more time you can spend each day appreciating what you have and where you are, the more open you are to change.

Creating a Ritual

In summary, these are the steps you should take.

Empower your talisman and the sigil you plan to use.

Get everything ready to begin your working on a Thursday.

Write down your request. You may find it beneficial to write out the entire ritual.

Face East. Place the Shem Talisman before you, with the chosen angelic sigil ready to hand.

Perform the Master Ritual, using the imagination techniques you have learned, empowering the work with your feelings, as you read out your request.

Perform the ritual once a day for eleven days, at any time you like, completing the working on a Sunday.

Let go and know that it is done and that results will come.

Do all you can to make the result come about, opening the doors to magickal manifestation, without lusting for results.

The 72 Angels of Magick

The following pages give you all the names, pronunciations, sigils and chants you need, along with a list of all the angels' powers.

You will notice that many of the names appear similar, so how can you tell them apart? Each angel has a different sigil, a different Hebrew spelling, a different pronunciation and a different list of powers.

Although the similarity of the names may be confusing at times, you will come to recognize the individual angels and their powers as you read about them.

The Powers of Vehuiah

To Carry Out a Difficult Task

Useful when you are trying to complete a task, but have faced many difficulties. Also useful when you are worried that a task will be difficult, because you feel the task stretches your abilities. Ideal for tasks that are wearing you out, and that feel impossible to complete.

To Strengthen Your Will

If you feel your willpower fading in general, you can use this angel to strengthen your will. Also ideal for strengthening your will to complete a task, or to help you stick to a promise or resolution. If you're trying to give up a habit or develop a new, positive habit, this angel will help.

To Obtain Esteem

Many angels can help with esteem, but this angel is best used when you want to increase your self-esteem and have that improvement be perceived by others. This makes you appear more confident and in control. This is also an excellent angel for improving your own sense of charisma, enabling you to seem charismatic to others.

Pronounced: VEH-WHO-EE-AH

Invocation (Psalm 3:3)

VEH-AH-TAH EE-AH-OH-EH MAH-GEN
BAH-AH-DEE KEH-VAW-DEE
OO-MAY-REEM RAW-SHE

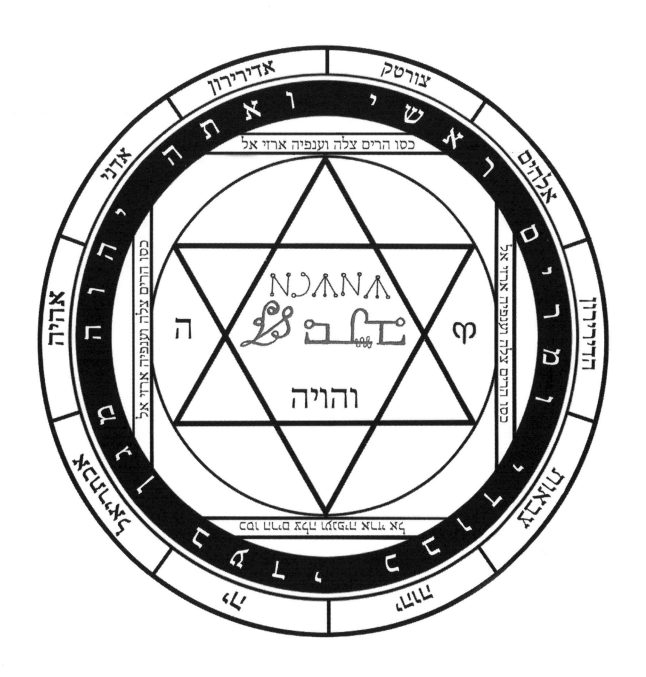

Vehuiah

VEH-WHO-EE-AH

The Powers of Yeliel

To Create Passionate Sex

When you want to increase the passion between yourself and your current partner, this angel can help. You can perform the ritual with or without the knowledge of your partner and the passion will increase. This can be used when your sex life has become dull or infrequent, or if you want to expand your sex life into more adventurous areas.

To Bring Calm Between Arguing Lovers

This angel can be used on your own relationship, when you find yourselves arguing all the time. If arguments seem to be weighing down an otherwise healthy relationship, or the arguments are becoming more aggressive than healthy arguments should be, this is the ideal angel. You can also use this angel to calm other couples you know, if they are arguing. This is especially useful if you have loud, arguing neighbors.

To Attract Love

You can use this angel to improve your chances of attracting love. If you have a particular person in mind, this is not the right angel, but if you want to improve the amount of love in your life, this is the way. You can use the angel to attract friends or lovers.

To Ensure Fidelity

If you sense that your partner may be seeking love elsewhere, this angel can reduce temptation. A side-effect of this can be that your partner feels a strong urge to tell you about the feelings of infidelity. This can potentially harm, end or heal a relationship, so proceed carefully. You can also use this angel on others. If you sense that your parents, for example, may be indulging in relationships outside of their partnership, you could use this angel to discourage the infidelity, to restore their love and focus on each other.

Pronounced: YEH-LEE-ELL

Invocation (Psalm 22:19)

VEH-AH-TAH EE-AH-OH-EH AHL
TEER-CHAK AY-AL-OH-TEE
LEH-EZ-RAH-TEE CHOO-SHAH

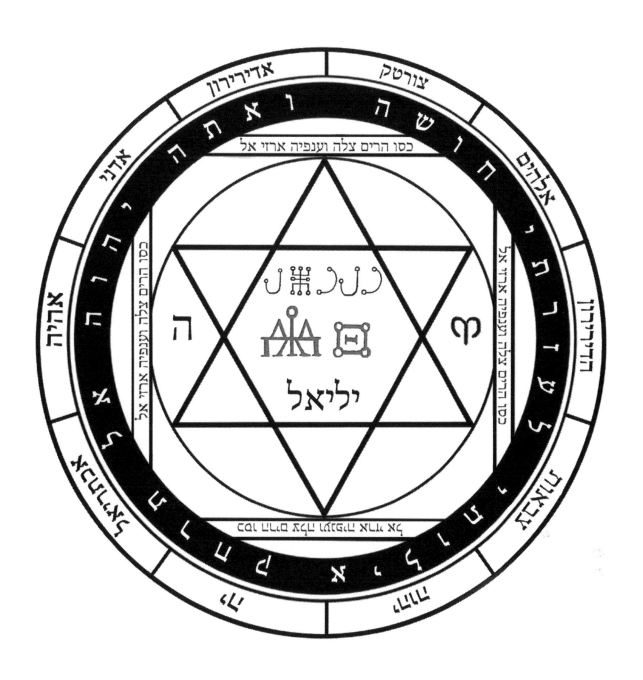

Yeliel

YEH-LEE-ELL

The Powers of Sitael

To Protect Against Adversity

If you have been experiencing a time of extended misfortune that's made you wonder whether you're cursed, this angel can reverse the misfortune. If you are in real danger from somebody you know - either physical or emotional danger - this is also a good angel to employ. When times are hard, and you are struggling to get any of your projects to work, this angel can help to improve your luck.

To Discover Truth

There are times when you want to discover whether somebody is telling you the truth. If you suspect that somebody is lying to you, within a relationship, at work or in any other situation, use this angel to find out. The answer may come in the form of a confession, strong intuition or a dream.

To Stop Hypocrisy

People often say one thing and then do another. Most of the time, this is a minor annoyance, but if somebody's hypocrisy damages your life in some way, use this angel. If you have a friend that tells you not to gossip, but spreads gossip about you, this angel would be ideal. If you know somebody who complains about bad debtors, but never pays up, this is the angel you need. Within a relationship you can use this angel to calm an annoying trait in your partner.

To Find Employment

This angel is used by those looking for work, and good results are reported by those looking for a new job, a promotion or a complete change of career. Be clear about what sort of work you are looking for and you will see progress.

Pronounced: SIT-AH-ELL

Invocation (Psalm 91:2)

AWE-MAHR LAH-EE-OH-AH-EH
MAHCH-SEE OOM-ETS-OO-DAH-TEE
ELL-OH-HIGH EV-TACH BAW

Sitael

SIT-AH-ELL

The Powers of Elemiah

The Power to Stop Mental Torment

When you find that you are unable to relax or recover from a problem that leaves you anxious and preoccupied, this angel can bring relief. It can also ease pain after the loss of a loved one, and make it easier to get through a bad breakup, or the loss of a job.

The Power to Discover New Methods

When we do things the same way, year after year, it is only to be expected that we will get the same results. This angel can give you the power to discover new ways of doing things. This is best used when you already have a method for something in place, but want to find a better way. A lawyer, for example, may use this angel to find a new way to prepare for a case. A student might look for better ways to learn. If you work in business or sales, you might look for new methods of getting a good response from customers.

The Power to Travel Safely

Many angels protect you when travelling, but this angel is best used when you are the leader of a group or family. It will ensure that whatever problems occur during your journey, you will be able to guide those you lead, with all being protected until the journey is over. Complete the working on the last Sunday before your journey commences.

Pronounced: ELL-EM-EE-AH

Invocation (Psalm 34:15)

EH-NAY EE-AH-OH-EH
EL TSAH-DEE-KEEM
VEH-AWES-NAHV ELL
SHAH-VUH-AH-TAHM

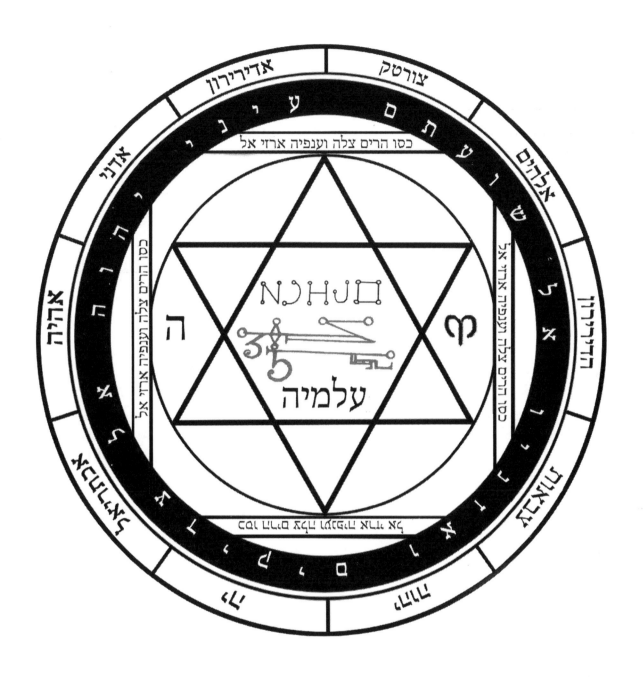

Elemiah

ELL-EM-EE-AH

The Powers of Mahasiah

The Power to Bring Peace

Using the power of this angel you can bring peace to a particular location, such as a workplace, a home or even an entire street. When people are in conflict in a specific area, ask this angel to subdue anger and aggression in that place.

The Power to Learn Like a Genius

Whether you're studying for an exam, learning a new skill or simply developing your personal skills, this angel can make you learn with the same abilities as a genius. This angel is also useful when you are learning a complex physical skill, such as learning to drive, sail, or fly an airplane.

The Power to Overcome Disease

If you have a long-term illness, this angel can help you cope with the symptoms, and some say it can help reverse the effects of the illness. This should not be used for injuries or short-term illnesses such as flu, but for illnesses that have affected you for months and show no sign of improvement.

Pronounced: MAH-HA-SHE-AH

Invocation (Psalm 80:19)

EE-AH-OH-EH ELL-OH-HEEM
TZEH-VAH-OUGHT
HAH-SHE-VAY-NOO
HA-AYER PAH-NE-CHA
VEH-KNEE-VAH-SHAY-AH

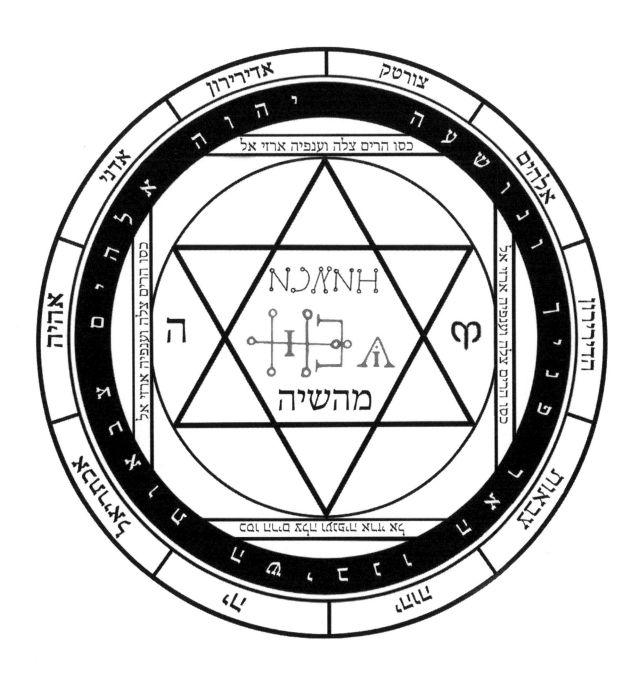

Mahasiah

MAH-HA-SHE-AH

The Powers of Lelahel

To Inspire Love in Another

When you want somebody to love you, this is the angel that can help. This works even when the person barely knows you or has shown no previous interest, but only if your intention is to seek a loving relationship, rather than a mere seduction or casual fling. Don't sit back and wait for the potential lover to seek you out, but notice any changes in their attitude and then act to develop the love between the two of you.

To Attract Fame Through Talents

If you are trying to become famous through a particular talent, this angel will help. The angel is especially suited to artistic talents, so if you are a writer, musician or artist, you can ask for your talents to be recognized more widely. This angel will not necessarily earn you more money or improve your career, but can make you better known because of your particular talent.

To Increase Luck in Relation to Ambition

If you have strong ambition in any area, whether artistic, financial or personal, this angel will bring you improved luck to help you achieve your ambition.

Inspiration for Artists

Most artists suffer from blockages when inspiration fails to strike. If you are going through one of these times, seek help from this angel and allow yourself to create experimentally. The results are extremely powerful.

Pronounced: LEH-LAH-ELL

Invocation (Psalm 86:3)

CHAH-NAY-KNEE EE-AH-OH-EH
KEY AIL-ECH-AH EKUH-RAH
KOL HA-YAWM

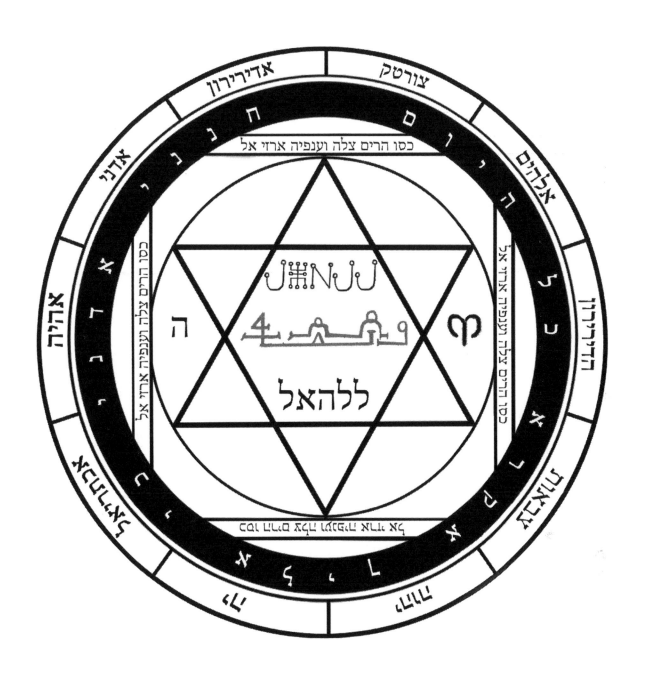

Lelahel

LEH-LAH-ELL

The Powers of Achaiah

To Make Your Work or Business Popular

This angel will help spread the word about your business, making it more popular. If you are employed, it will make your work within the organization more widely recognized.

Turn Enemies into Friends

When you have an enemy, the temptation is often to silence, bind or harm them with magick, but it's worth considering the option of turning an enemy into a friend. If you can open yourself to this possibility, the angel will respond.

Pronounced: AH-CHAH-EE-AH

Invocation (Psalm 3:5)

AH-NEE SHAH-CHAHV-TEE
VAH-EESH-AH-NAH
HECK-EAT-ZORE-TEA
KEY EE-AH-OH-EH
YEES-MUH-CHAY-NEE

Achaiah

AH-CHAH-EE-YAH

The Powers of Cahetel

The Power to Drive Away Evil

There are many forms of evil in the world, and most are human, but if you live or work in a place that is plagued by evil spirits, this angel can drive them away. It will even work to protect you from demons, if somebody has cursed you using demonic powers.

The Power to Create a Strong Voice

This is one of those powers that many people will ignore, but it remains one of the most useful. Although it has clear use for politicians, public speakers and actors, it can be used by anybody to give a voice more presence. This means you are more likely to be heard when you speak, and so long as you choose your words carefully, this can make many doors open for you.

The Power to Control Growth in Nature

If you grow plants, or work with crops, this angel can help to ensure that you will get good results from your efforts.

Pronounced: CAH-HET-ELL

Invocation (Psalm 119:75)

YAH-DAH-AH-TEE EE-AH-OH-EH
KEY TSED-ECK
MEESH-PAH-TECH-AH
VAY-EH-MOON-AH
EE-NEAT-AH-KNEE

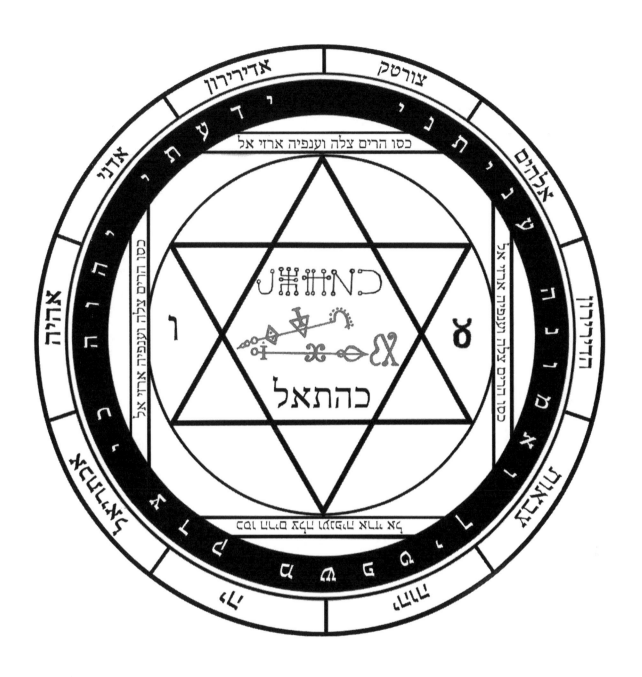

Cahetel

CAH-HET-ELL

The Powers of Heziel

To Obtain Friendship of the Great

Use this angel if you want to be well liked by your boss or any superior. This angel is particularly useful if you are trying to be recognized or appreciated by figures who are normally difficult to impress – such as literary agents, publishers and other gatekeepers of the creative arts. When you want to rise through the ranks of an organization, this angel can ensure you are seen and liked by those at the top.

Make Somebody Fulfill a Promise

When somebody makes a promise of any kind, and then fails to follow through, use this angel to make them fulfill the promise. This works well when you are owed money, but is valuable in personal and professional situations as well.

Protect Against Hidden Enemies

If you sense that somebody is undermining your efforts, either at work or in your relationships, use this angel to protect yourself. The angel will ensure that your enemy's efforts are wasted.

Pronounced: HEZ-EE-ELL

Invocation (Psalm 88:14)

LAH-MAH EE-AH-OH-EH
TEASE-NACH
NAHF-SHE TAH-STEER
PAH-NEH-CHAH ME-MEN-EE

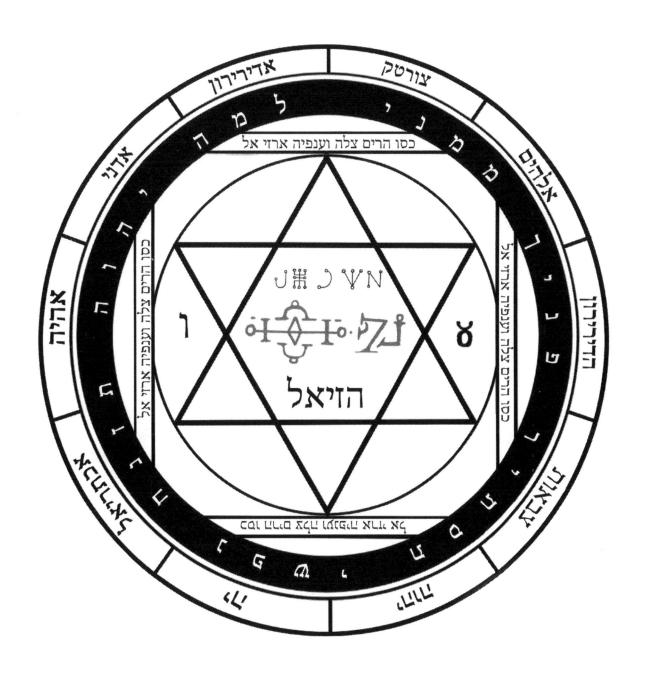

Heziel

HEZ-EE-ELL

The Powers of Eladiah

The Power to Heal Disease

To say that an angel can cure disease is a mighty claim, and one that risks giving people false hope, but Eladiah has a reputation for helping people with bone and joint problems. If you have a long-term problem that you want to ease, or a recent injury that you want to heal, call on Eladiah to ease your suffering.

The Power to Overcome Negativity

If you are surrounded by negative people, or negative responses to your work, call on this angel. Close relationships often succumb to excessive negativity, and this angel can ease the friction between a couple. If you find that your own responses to the world are negative, the angel can help you to see situations with more clarity.

The Power to Understand Science

This angel is used to obtain a deep understanding of a scientific subject. If you are studying a complex scientific subject, this angel can help you to understand new information and remember it with clarity. It is particularly useful for science that has clear practical applications, such as medical science.

Pronounced: EH-LAH-DEE-AH

Invocation (Psalm 88:1)

EE-AH-OH-EH ELL-OH-HAY
YEH-SHOO-AH-TEA
YAWM TSAH-AHK-TEA
BAH-LIE-LAH
NEG-DEH-CHA

Eladiah

EH-LAH-DEE-YAH

The Powers of Laviah

The Power to Find True Followers
Not everybody needs a fan base, but many people do, especially now that even cafes and parking lots have their own online presence. If you have a public profile of any kind, and need followers or friends, this is the angel to call upon. If you require support or votes in any kind of campaign, the angel can help. It works best when you are looking for sincere followers who will help and get involved, rather than large numbers of casual followers.

The Power to Overcome Enemies
This angel can overcome many enemies, but is best suited at calming the jealous. If somebody you know is damaging your life through jealousy, call on this angel to calm the situation. Rather than punishing your enemy or putting fear in their heart, this angel works by making the other person less jealous of you. They may even lose interest in your affairs completely.

The Power to Find Fame Through Talent
If you have a talent that is recognized by a small group, but you struggle to achieve wider recognition, call on this angel. It's important that your talent has already been acknowledged by a few people (other than friends or family) before you call on the angel. This is ideal for a struggling writer, for example, who has published a few stories but remains relatively unknown. It is best used when you are about to launch a new project into the world.

The Power to Influence the Famous
If you ever need to influence somebody of great fame or renown, call on this angel. Laviah can influence the thoughts and actions of those who are well known. This doesn't just apply to movie stars – you can use this angel to influence politicians, leaders of companies and other public figures. You should only use this angel when you have already established some form of contact with the person in question.

Pronounced: LAH-VEE-AH

Invocation (Psalm 27:13)

LOO-LAY HEH-EH-MAHN-TEA
LEAR-AUGHT BEH-TOOV
EE-AH-OH-EH BEH-EH-RETZ CHAH-YEEM

Laviah

LAH-VEE-AH

The Powers of Hahaiah

The Power to Overcome Adversity

Some angels help you endure adversity, but this angel helps you stop it. When you are faced with an adverse situation, the angel can help you to escape from it, or bring it to a halt, and you should make it clear which option you prefer when writing your request. If, for example, you are experiencing stress at work, you should make it clear that you want the stress to be relieved, not that you want to leave your job. Unless you do want to leave your job. This angel has immense power, and can be used against all kinds of adversity, from a difficult divorce to difficult legal problems.

The Power to Make Enemies into Friends

There are some people that you cannot remove from your life, but who make you miserable. Whether they attack you directly or not, if such people make you miserable, you can call on this angel to make them friendlier.

The Power to Find Mystical Answers in Dreams

When you want the answer to a question, call on this angel to give you prophetic dreams. You can seek answers about your future, your self, your true nature and desires, or the best path to take.

Pronounced: HAH-HAH-EE-AH

Invocation (Psalm 6:4)

SHOO-VAH EE-AH-OH-EH
CHAH-LEH-TZAH
NAHF-SHE HAW-SHE-AIN-EE
LEH-MAH-AHN CHAS-DEH-CHAH

Hahaiah

HAH-HAH-EE-AH

The Powers of Yezelel

Inspires Writers and Artists

Many angels are useful to artists, but this particular angel is beneficial when you are already working on a project, but need a boost of inspiration to improve the project or see it through to completion.

Reunites Lovers

This angel can be used to bring back the attraction and friendship of a relationship. You can use this angel on a failing relationship, on a lover who has left you, or a lover that you left. The angel will not heal the problems that caused the separation in the first place, so be prepared to work on the relationship once it begins again.

Passing Exams and Tests

This angel helps you to pass exams and tests of any kind. The key the getting this to work is to begin the magick long before the test, because the angel helps with understanding and memory, making you more capable of passing the test.

Learn The Plans of an Enemy

When you suspect that an enemy is making plans, you need to find out what they are planning. There is no more powerful weapon than information, so use this to see how somebody is planning to harm you. This can even be used on non-enemies; if you have a competitor in business, you can learn their plans through this angel. The answer may come in dreams, through coincidences or through gossip and revelations made by others.

Pronounced: YEH-ZELL-ELL

Invocation (Psalm 104:16)

YEES-BEH-OO AH-TSAY
EE-AH-OH-EH
AHR-ZAY LEH-VAH-NAWN
AH-SHARE NAH-TAH

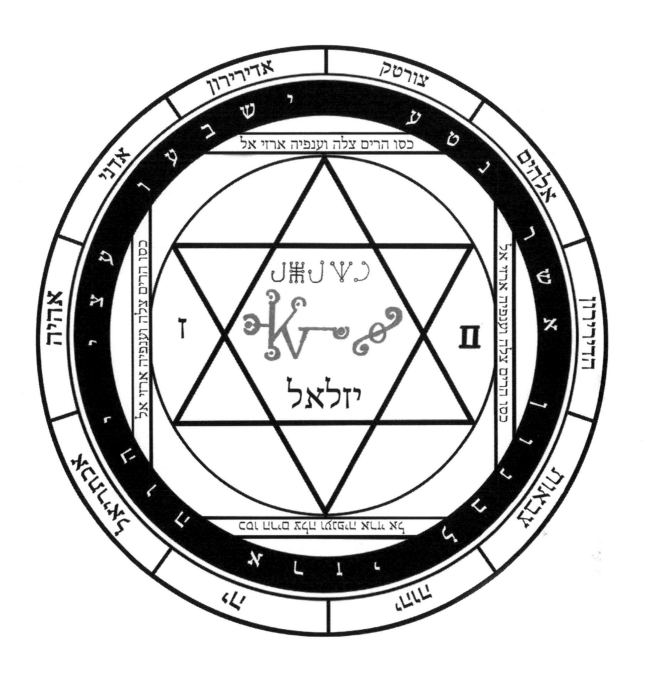

Yezelel

YEH-ZELL-ELL

The Powers of Mebahel

The Power to Save a Just Cause

If you are fighting a cause that you believe to be just – whether it is a public protest or a campaign to raise funds – call on this angel when it feels like defeat is near. The angel will give new energy and impetus to your cause.

The Power to Avoid Injustice During a Trial

If you need to avoid injustice during court proceedings, call on this angel. If you are guilty in any way, do not call on this angel, because it will ensure justice is done.

The Power to Reveal Enemies

Knowing your enemy can be the key to defeating them. If you sense that you are being attacked, slandered or undermined, call on this angel to reveal those who are against you. Your enemy may be revealed through a dream, intuition, or when your enemy makes a clear declaration, or even by forcing your enemy to make a revealing error.

Pronounced: MEB-AH-ELL

Invocation (Psalm 9:9)

VEE-HEE EE-AH-OH-EH
MEES-GAHV
LAH-DAHCH
MEES-GAHV
LEH-EE-TAUT BATZ-AH-RAH

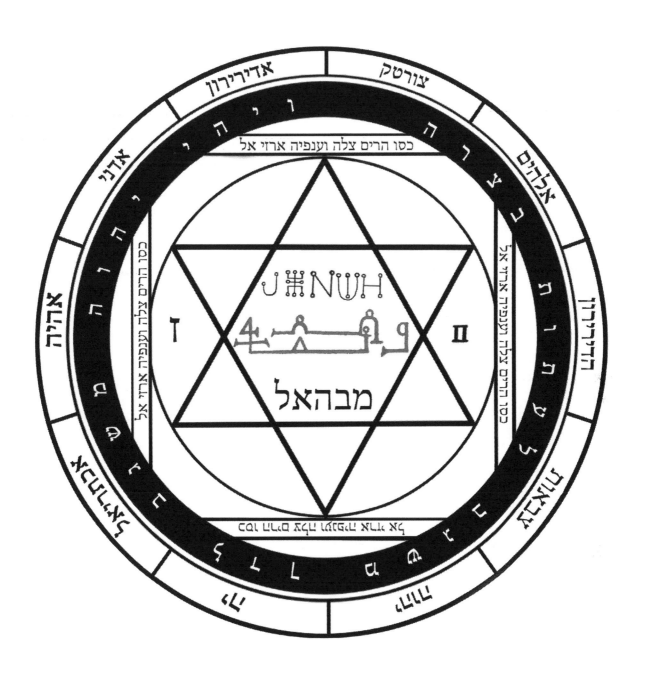

Mebahel

MEB-AH-ELL

The Powers of Hariel

The Power to Bring Peace to Your Home

This angel works best to make your home peaceful when the disruption comes from within the home (rather than due to troublesome neighbors). If there are ongoing arguments, disputes and fights within your home, or just a bad atmosphere, this is the angel you should call on to bring peace.

The Power to Improve Magickal Power

Hariel can increase the energy you put into all your magickal workings. You should call on the angel to improve your magickal power generally, and watch your abilities increase over the coming year.

The Power to Discover a Peaceful Pathway

We are constantly facing choices about which way to go with our lives. Sometimes you want success and money at any cost. At other times, all you want is peace. If you are seeking a period of time where life is more peaceful, without it actually wrecking your career or reputation, ask this angel to show you the way. You may discover new opportunities or simply get an intuition about how best to proceed.

Pronounced: HAH-REE-ELL

Invocation (Psalm 128:4)

HEE-NAIH KEY
CHEN YEH-VAW-RAHCH
GAH-VER YEH-RAY
EE-AH-OH-EH

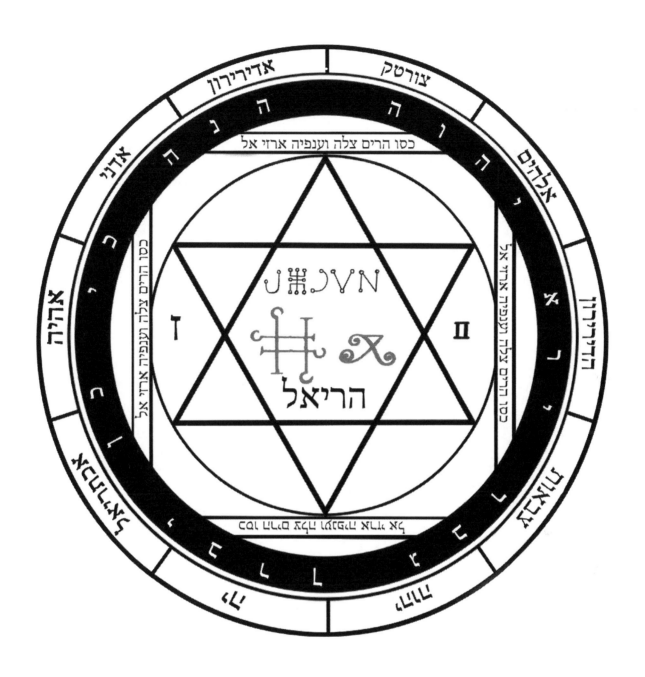

Hariel

HAH-REE-ELL

The Powers of Hakemiah

The Power to Stop Traitors

Wherever you work closely with other people, there is the potential for betrayal. This can occur within an organization, a group of friends or in business. If you suspect that a traitor is in your midst, this angel will reveal the truth. The traitor may do something that reveals the truth, or you may get a strong intuition, or a message in a dream that reveals how this person is undermining your life.

The Power to Stop Oppressors

If somebody is holding you back, or oppressing your ability to express the life you want to lead, this angel can take that person's power away. This angel can be used in domestic situations, or in large-scale corporations, against individuals or large groups of people.

The Power to Acquire Dignity and Prosperity

Any angel that promises prosperity is hugely appealing to magickal workers, but be aware that this angel works by bringing prosperity through improved dignity. In other words, the angel will make you appear more dignified and appealing to people, so that you are more likely to be hired, be awarded a position or have your business become more popular. For this angel to work, you must be somebody who interacts with people in the place where you make money. It is ideal for everybody from retail workers and laborers, to people who speak to large groups, but is not ideal for people who work remotely, such as those who run an online business.

Pronounced: HAH-KEM-EE-AH

Invocation (Psalm 10:1)

LAH-MAH EE-AH-OH-EH
TAH-AH-MAWD
BEH-RAH-CHOK
TAH-AH-LEEM LEH-EE-TAUGHT
BATZ-AH-RAH

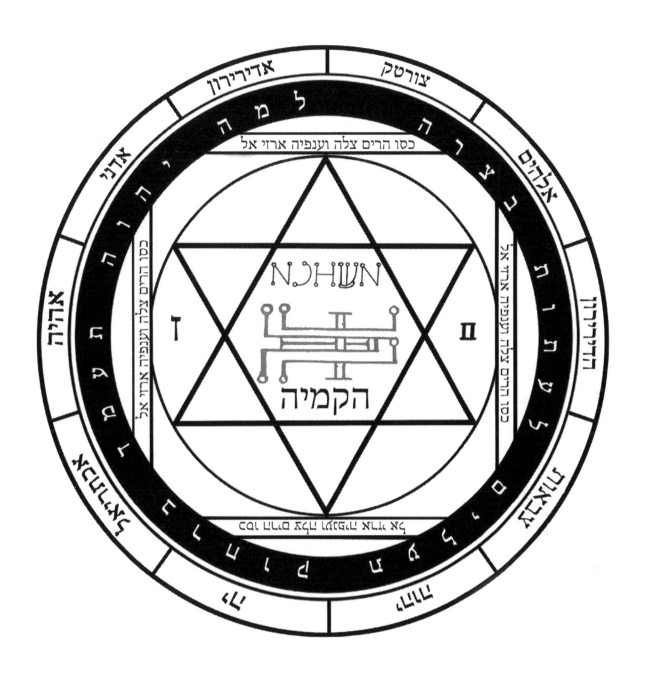

Hakemiah

HAH-KEM-EE-AH

The Powers of Lavel

The Power to Create Music

This angel helps musicians to create their own compositions. You may find that you discover new ways of composing music, or it could be that your skills and intuition combine so that you make greater creative choices.

The Power to Perform Music

Whether you perform music for pleasure or profit, this angel can ensure that you give an inspired performance. It can be used by performers recording in a studio, but the most dramatic effects are seen when used for live performance.

The Power to Overcome Sorrow and Torment

If you are struggling to get over a particular sadness, or if you are plagued by a memory that refuses to go away, call on this angel to ease your anguish.

The Power to Invent and Design with Genius

Whether you're designing buildings, apps or book covers, this angel can give you the inspiration to create in a new way. The angel works most effectively if you already have some competence or skill in an area of invention, and pushes you to create, invent and design like a genius.

Pronounced: LAH-VELL

Invocation (Psalm 105:1)

HAW-DO LAH EE-AH-OH-EH
KEH-ROO
VEESH-UMAW
HAW-DEE-OO
VAH-AH-MEEM
AH-LEE-LAW-TAHV

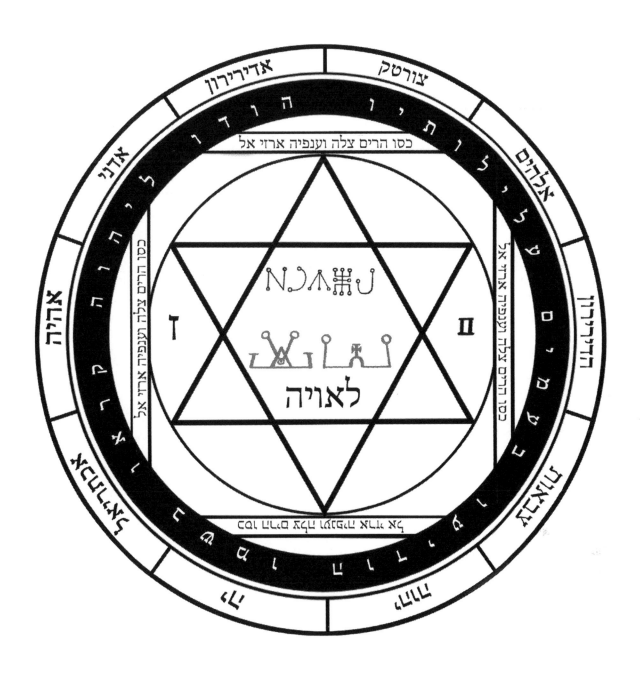

Lavel

LAH-VELL

The Powers of Keliel

The Power to Avoid Enemies

There are times when you want to defeat or overcome an enemy, and other times when it is wiser to work in the background, out of sight, so that you can overcome the enemy at a later time. If you need this power, Keliel can make sure you do not encounter your enemies while you make your plans. This works even if you are unsure who your enemies are.

The Power to Become Less Visible

Sometimes you want to lie low, and not be noticed by others. If you feel the need to disappear from the world for a while, call on this angel to make you less visible. This works on a physical level (so people will not see you clearly), and prevents people from thinking about you or remembering you. Tell the angel how long you want the effect to last. If you change your mind and want it to end sooner, perform the ritual for one day (on any day), but change your request, asking the angel to reverse your request.

The Power to Confuse Enemies

This power works best against those who say false things about you, or people who try to distract you from your life and work. When your enemies think about you, they will experience confusion, making them unwilling to fight you, and making it easier for you to defeat them.

Pronounced: KEH-LEE-ELL

Invocation (Psalm 103:21)

BAH-REH-CHOO
EE-AH-OH-EH KAWL
TZEH-VAH-AHV
MEH-SHAH-REH-TAHV
AWES-AY REH-TZAW-NAW

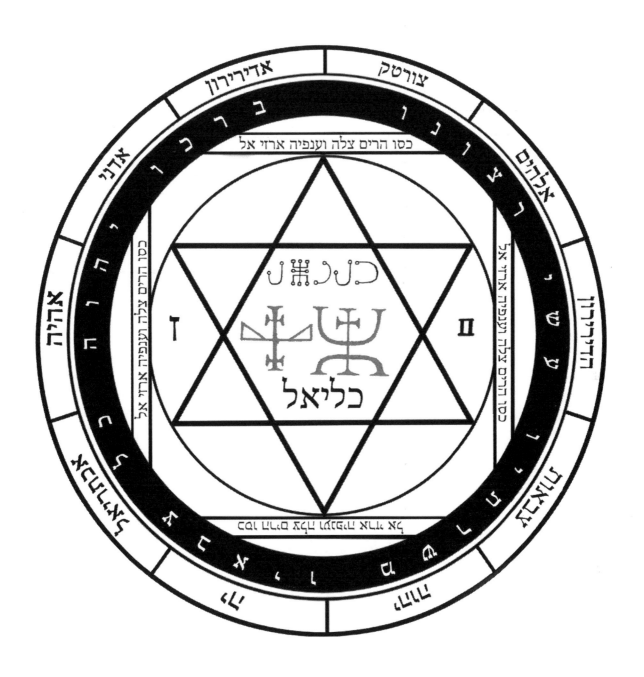

Keliel

KEH-LEE-ELL

The Powers of Lovel

The Power to Generate Love in Another

This angel can make a person that likes you love you, but this is not an angel of seduction; this magick only works when there is potential for love. If you feel love for somebody, this angel helps the person you desire sense your love. When there is any potential for a relationship, this effect of sensing your love can move the person to feel more love for you.

The Power to Be Loved by Friends and Enemies

If you feel that your friends are lukewarm toward you, or take you for granted, call on this angel to gain their love. The angel will not make friends love you more than they did before, but it will make them remember and feel the love they have for you. When used on enemies, it will cause the other person to be confused by the change in their feelings.

The Power to Make Good Decisions

This probably doesn't sound like a spectacular power, but it is one of the most important in the book. We make thousands of small decisions every day, but sometimes we are faced with difficult choices. When you are struggling to decide on the next course of action, this angel can help you to sense your own true will and get a sense for how the future will manifest.

The Power to Obtain Good Memory and Intelligence

For anybody struggling with memory, this angel is an excellent way to recover your faculties. This angel is also good when you are learning a new subject. It is good at creating long-term understanding, so it should be used when you are learning rather than at the last minute before an exam.

Pronounced: LAW-VUH-ELL

Invocation (Psalm 40:1)

CAH-VAWH KEY-VEE-TEE
EE-AH-OH-EH VAH-EE-YET
EH-LIE VAH-YEESH-MAH
SHAH-VUH-AH-TEE

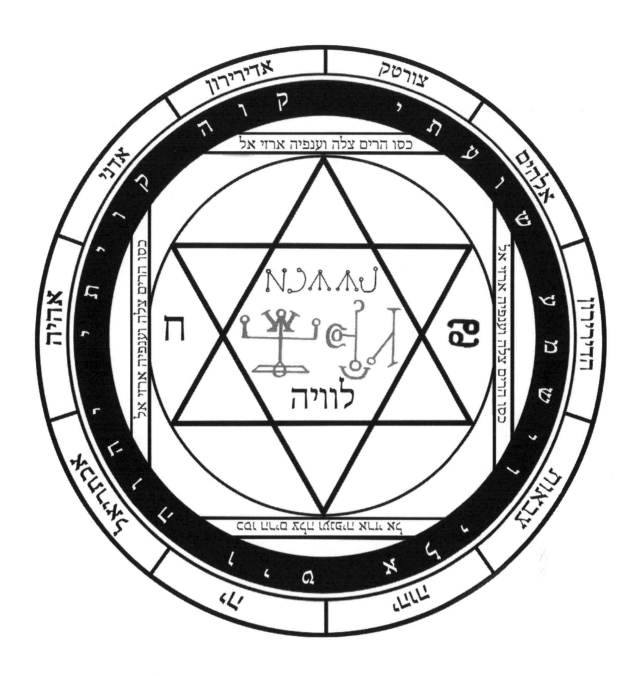

Lovel

LAW-VUH-ELL

The Powers of Pahaliah

The Power to Find Balance

How often do we hear people saying that they have no balance in their life? Usually this is because people are overworked and not able to spend enough time with family, but it can also occur for other reasons. If you feel that your life lacks balance, and you want to discover a long-term solution call on this angel to open up new opportunities that will bring more balance into your life.

The Power to Experience Joy

Even when things are going well you may find that you feel down, or unimpressed with the world. If you want to enjoy the life you are already living, and throw off your doubts and fears, this angel will help you to live in the moment.

The Power to Find a Spiritual Path

When magick begins to work, you may find yourself wondering whether or not you deserve these results. This is a common reaction, and many people stop working magick after a few positive results, because they feel they have an unfair advantage. An alternative solution is to know that magick is part of your spiritual journey. Call on this angel to give you insights into where you should go from here.

Pronounced: PAH-HAH-LEE-AH

Invocation (Psalm 119:108)

KNEE-DEH-VAWT PEA REH-TZAY
NAH EE-AH-OH-EH
OOM-EESH-PAH-TECH-AH
LAH-MEH-DAY-KNEE

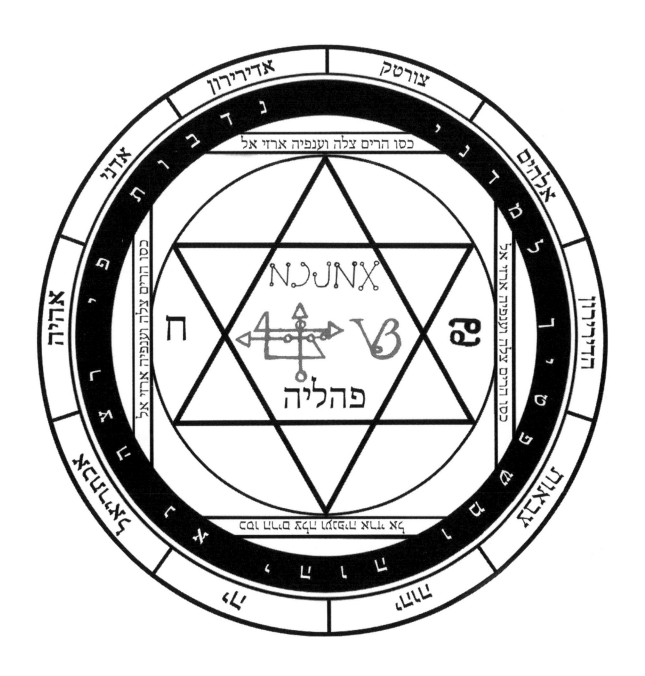

Pahaliah

PAH-HAH-LEE-AH

The Powers of Nelachel

The Power to Stop Slander

Gossip can be harmless but when it turns to slander, the effects on your life can be extremely negative. This angel can stop slander, even if you're not sure who is telling stories about you. In legal terms, slander refers to people telling untruths about you, but this angel will also stop people from repeating true stories about you if they are damaging to your reputation.

The Power to Subdue Negativity

If you are feeling negative about life in general, or a specific area of your life, this angel will work to ease your negative thoughts. Sometimes, negative thoughts are beneficial as they help you to make reasoned judgments. When negativity becomes habitual, though, it can lead to you missing opportunities. The angel works by brightening your mood, and can even remove the cause of your negative mood, whether you know what the cause is or not.

The Power to Make Calculations

If you ever work with numbers, this angel can make you an expert. Pilots, engineers and scientists will find it easier to make accurate mental calculations using the power of this angel. If you are a student who struggles with math, the angel can make your work easier. Call on this angel for eleven days, and the effects can last for many years.

Pronounced: NELL-AH-CHELL

Invocation (Psalm 18:49)

AHL CANE AWE-DEH-CHAH
BAH-GAW-YEEM
EE-AH-OH-EH
OOL-SHEE-MUH-CHAH
AH-ZAH-MAY-RAH

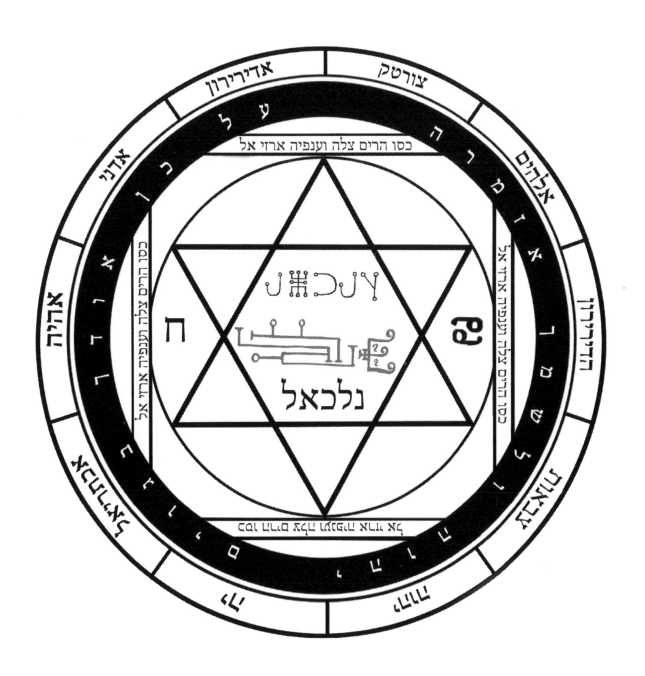

Nelachael

NELL-AH-CHELL

The Powers of Yeyayel

Wealth, Fame and Success

This angel can help to promote wealth, fame and success, especially when you are working on all three aspects at once. If your success does not involve some level of fame or notoriety, then you may prefer to use a different angel. When your business, work or art involves fame and the potential to make money, this is the angel you need. If you are working on a career that requires fame, but have not yet achieved any, this angel can help to get you known.

Protection While Travelling

Before you travel – whether for work or pleasure - ask for protection from this angel, to save you from physical harm, robbery, illness or anything else you fear while travelling.

Good Luck When Making Deals

If you're selling a house, or trying to sign a contract of any kind, this is the angel you want. It helps when you've already got somebody interested in your project, and you're at the point where you're negotiating a contract. This can work for any project where you're negotiating a deal. It works for all aspects of negotiation, not just the financial side. Whatever deal you are working on, your luck will be improved.

Pronounced: YEH-YAH-EE-ELL

Invocation (Psalm147:11):

RAW-TZEH EE-AH-OH-EH
ET YEH-RAY-AHV
ET HAHM-YAH-CHAH-LEEM
LEH-CHAS-DAW

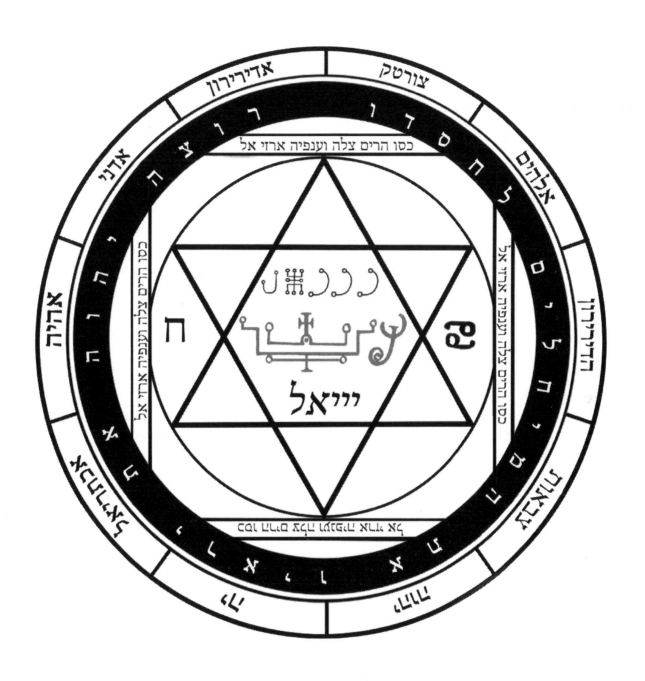

Yeyayel

YEH-YAH-EE-ELL

The Powers of Melahel

The Power to Travel Safely

Many angels give you the power to travel safely, but this one is especially useful if you are travelling through an area with many weapons. This can be used by soldiers and civilians travelling in war zones.

The Power to Defend Against Weapons

This power is similar to that above, but is aimed specifically at people who are in danger from weapons when they are not travelling. This is more useful if you live or work in an area where weapons are carried, or where weapons are commonly being used illegally.

To Heal Illness and Injury

This angel can heal illness and injury, so long as you have the energy to perform the ritual. It is not useful when you are bedridden or weak. If you have an illness or injury that irritates you, or makes life difficult, this angel can ease your distress. The best results come when the illness or injury was acquired within recent weeks.

Pronounced: MEH-LAH-ELL

Invocation (Psalm 118:24)

ZEH HAH-YAWM
AH-SAH EE-AH-OH-EH
NAH-GEE-LAH
VUH-NEES-MUH-CHAH VAW

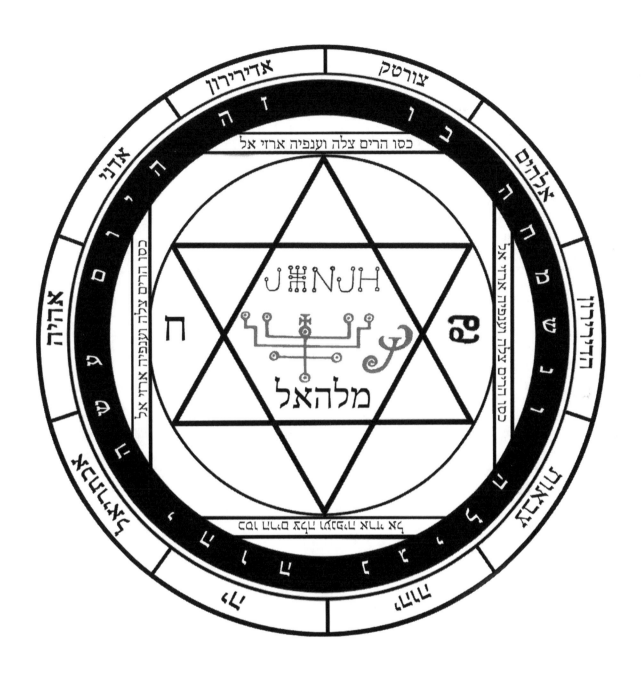

Melahel

MEH-LAH-ELL

The Powers of Chahuiah

The Power to Repel Thieves

Whether you want to protect your home from burglary, your self from being mugged or your business from thieves, this angel can bring you the protection you need. Call on the angel for eleven days, and the effects last for over a year.

The Power to Repel Pests

This is a power that I thought might be irrelevant in the modern world, until a friend reported a rat problem to me a few years ago. The building where she lived was infested with rats. Despite the fact that the people who owned the building should have dealt with the rats, they didn't do an effective job. By calling on this angel, the building was freed of rats. If there are pests in the area, this angel can protect your house before they get in. If your house is infested, use modern methods first, but if those methods fail, call on this angel to be free of any pest.

The Power to Develop Magick

This power will help you to work out what magick to use to get the result you want. If you know the end result you want, tell the angel and ask for understanding of the magick you need to use. As you read and study magick, it will become clear to you what methods you should use. You will also get an idea of when to use particular rituals and techniques, and in what order. This is useful when you have a complex, long-term goal that needs a many-pronged magickal approach.

Pronounced: CHAH-WHO-EE-AH

Invocation (Psalm 95:6)

BAW-OO NEESH-TAH-CHAH-VEH
VEH-NEE-CHUH-RAH-AH
NEEVE-REH-CHAH
LEAF-NAY
EE-AH-OH-EH
AWE-SAY-NOO

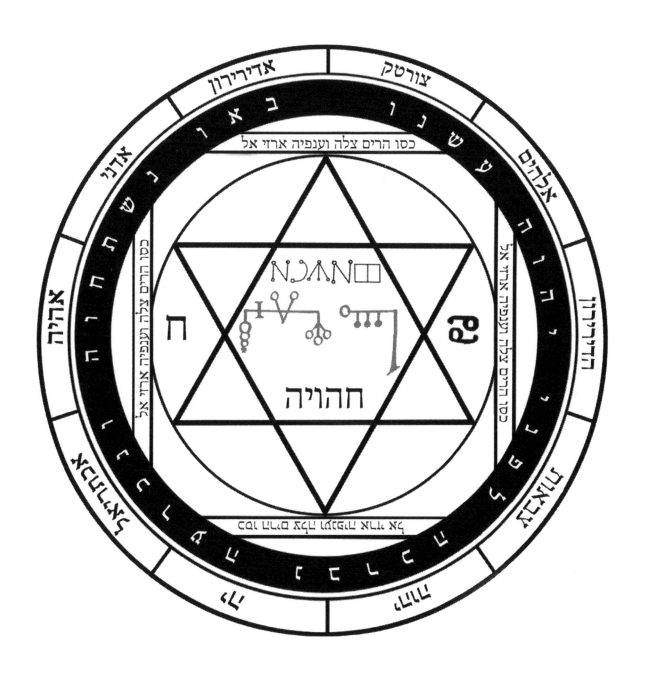

Chahuiah

CHAH-WHO-EE-AH

The Powers of Netahiah

Give Power to Magick

If you're using any other magick, from my books or elsewhere, use this angel to bring extra power to your magick. Sometimes there are blockages that prevent magick from working. The angel may remove them or make you aware of changes you need to make to get the magick working. Use this when magick isn't going the way you want, or if you're working on a ritual of extreme significance to you.

Discover Hidden Secrets

This angel can be used in two ways. If you know that something is being hidden from you, ask this angel to bring the information to you. Secondly, it can be used when you are trying to learn more about a particular person, company or situation. This sort of intelligence gathering is often neglected by occultists, but it can be more important to know the secrets that surround a situation than to attack a problem blindly.

Reveal Truth in Dreams

Sometimes it is difficult to discover the truth about a situation, and even when there is evidence in front of you, it can be impossible for you to be certain about what's going on. When you need to know the truth about something, ask this angel to reveal the truth in a dream. The angel does not predict the future, but will reveal the truth to you about any current situation, or somebody's thoughts and intentions.

Pronounced: NET-AH-EE-AH

Invocation (Psalm 34:4)

DAH-RAHSH-TEE ET
EE-AH-OH-EH VEH-AHN-AHN-EE
OOM-EE-KOL MEH-GOO-RAW-TAY
HE-TZEEL-AH-NEE

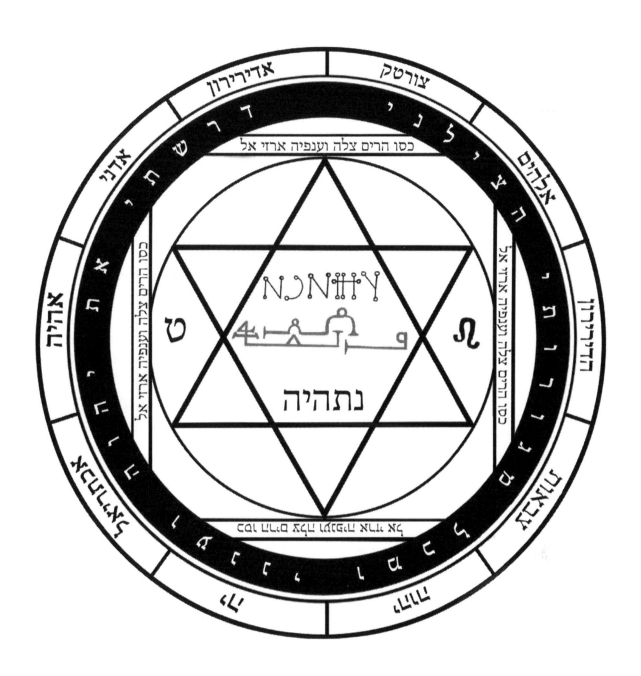

Netahiah

NET-AH-EE-YA

The Powers of Haaiah

The Power to Get a Fair Judgment

This angel won't get you out of trouble if you're guilty, but if you want a fair judgment in any matter, this is a powerful angel to have on your side. It can work in legal cases, but also if you're ever being judged in a work environment or even in a competition for an award.

The Power to Obtain Wealth Through Knowledge

For people who work in industries such as trading stocks or investing, this is the angel of choice as it can reveal knowledge that is not widely known, through intuition.

The Power to Arrange Trade Agreements

If you work in an industry that requires trade agreements, this angel will help. You might work in a market and be looking for a good deal from a wholesaler, or you might work in a large corporation that's seeking to make good overseas deals. Wherever agreements need to be made about trade, this angel will bring you excellent results.

The Power to Make Political Agreements

You don't have to be a politician to benefit from this angel, although many politicians do. This power can also be used in any situation that could be considered 'political'. If you're discussing matters with a committee, a board of directors, or any other group, this angel can help you to get the group to make decisions that are in accordance with your will.

Pronounced: HAH-AH-EE-AH

Invocation (Psalm 97:1)

EE-AH-OH-EH MAH-LAHCH
TAH-GAIL HA-AH-RETZ
YEES-MEH-CHOO
EE-YEEM RAH-BEAM

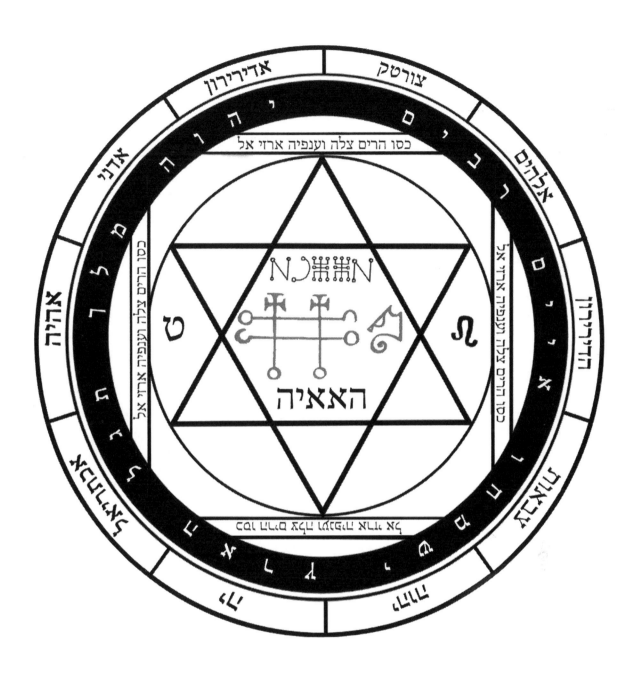

Haaiah

HAH-AH-EE-AH

The Powers of Yeretel

The Power to Write Well

The power of this angel is useful when writing essays for school, blog posts or books. It ensures that you write in a way that communicates your ideas with flair and precision. You can ask the angel to improve your writing skills generally, or aim the working at a specific project.

The Power to Find Fame Through Writing

If you find that you are able to write well, this angel can make your work more popular. If you are looking for an agent or publisher, this is not the best angel to use. This angel works best when there is already an outlet for your writing in place. Whether that is a blog, e-book or a traditional print book that's sold in the major bookshops, this angel will help make your writing more popular.

The Power to Spread Knowledge

If you want to spread knowledge, through writing, this angel will make your work easier. You may be launching a local protest, spreading news about a product, or even advertising your own services. So long as the knowledge you are sharing is true – as far as you know – this angel will help find outlets for your writing.

Pronounced: YEH-REH-TELL

Invocation (Psalm 140:1)

CHAH-LEH-TZAY-NEE
EE-AH-OH-EH MAY-AH-DAM
RAH MAY-EESH
CHAH-MAH-SEEM
TEEN-TZUH-RAY-NEE

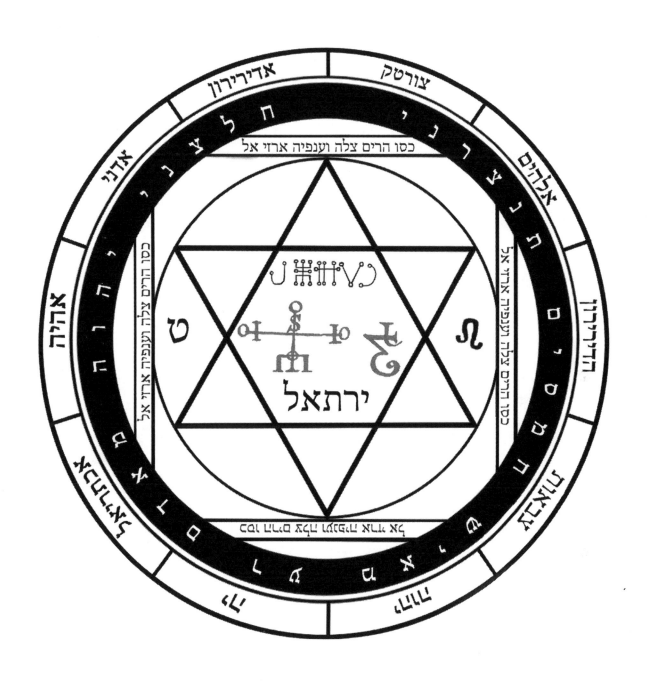

Yeretel

YEH-REH-TELL

The Powers of Shahahiah

The Power to Protect Against Disease

If there is an outbreak of disease where you live, or if you work in a hospital (or similar location) this angel can provide excellent protection against infection.

The Power to Maintain Health

People who practice gratitude notice their health on a daily basis, but many people say they only appreciate their health when they get sick. Preventative medicine is often the best medicine, so I recommend calling on this angel to maintain your health every few years. Only make this request when you feel in good health.

The Power to Protect Against Adverse Forces

This power is aimed at protecting you from natural disasters and other events that occur seemingly at random, rather than protecting you from conditions caused by enemies. Calling on an angel will not prevent a natural disaster, but it can help you weather the storm.

This power is used by people who live in earthquake zones or areas that suffer from cyclones and flooding, to reduce the adversity experienced during those events. It is best to use this as a preventative measure, because performing an eleven-day ritual when there's a nearby forest fire isn't much use. Once you've performed the ritual for prevention, however, you can call on the angel directly in an emergency. Simply gaze at the sigil, call for the angel and ask for protection – it only takes a moment to do so. (Only take the time to do this if it is genuinely safe to do so. If it's wiser to get in your car and escape, do that rather than the ritual.) If you live in an area that is prone to these disasters, perform the full ritual once every three years.

Pronounced: SHAH-AH-EE-AH

Invocation (Psalm 35:24)

SHAWF-TAY-NEE
CHUH-TZEE-DUH-KUH-CHAH
EE-AH-OH-EH ELL-AWE-HIGH
VEH-AHL YEES-MUH-CHOO LEE

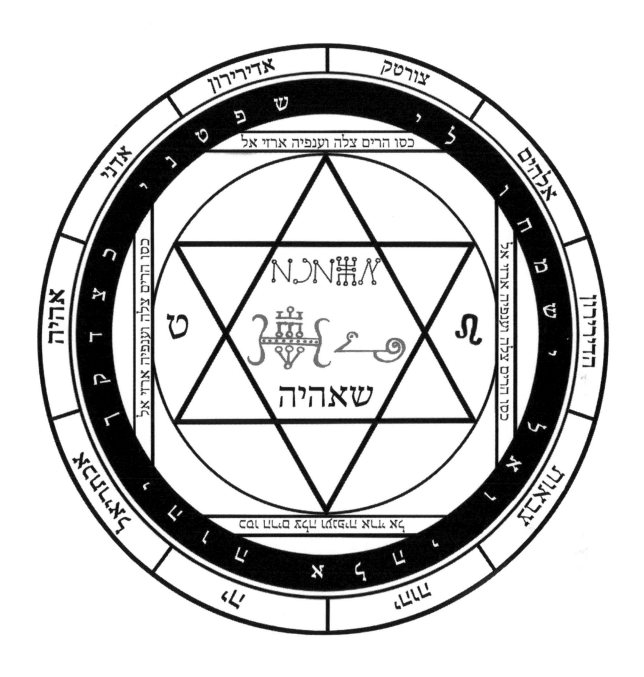

Shahahiah

SHAH-AH-EE-AH

The Powers of Riyiyel

The Power to Protect Against Hidden Enemies

Some enemies go to great lengths to disguise themselves. If you feel that you are being attacked by an unknown person or group, call on this angel to protect you from their actions.

The Power to Discover Secret Information

There are times when you need to know information that is hidden. This angel can reveal the plans of competitors, the secret thoughts of those close to you, and any other secret information that you feel would be valuable. In some cases, the information will appear out of the blue, or you will stumble across it. In other cases, you may receive a message in a dream, or get a strong intuition that guides you to know the secret.

Pronounced: REE-EE-ELL

Invocation (Psalm 9:11)

ZAH-MEH-ROO
LUH-EE-AH-OH-EE
YAW-SHEV TZEE-YAWN
HA-GEE-DOO
VAH-AH-MEEM
AH-LEE-LAW-TAHV

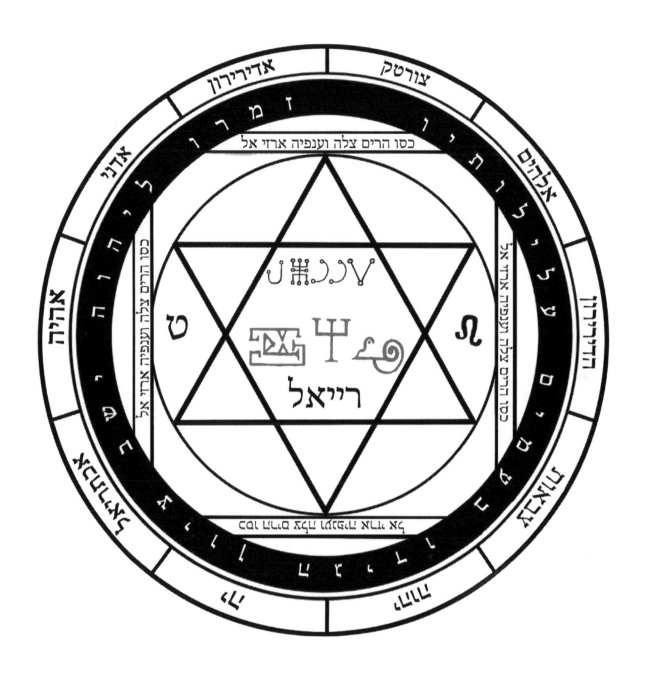

Riyiyel

REE-EE-ELL

The Powers of Omael

Willpower in The Face of Adversity

When you are working on anything, whether it's a personal project, an ambition, your job or a relationship, there are times when all you need is more willpower. When you are feeling exhausted by the challenges you face in any situation, use this angel to help give you the willpower to continue at your best.

Heal When You Have Failed

Failure is a normal part of success. Successful people experience constant failure, and the secret of success is to move on from the failures, learn from them and develop the successes. Sometimes, though, you fail in such a spectacular and hurtful way that you feel you can't recover. This angel can help you to heal when you have failed, whether the fault was yours or not.

Pronounced: AWE-MUH-ELL

Invocation (Psalm 7:17)

AWE-DEH EE-AH-OH-EH
KUH-TZEED-KAW
VAH-AH-ZAHM-RAH
SHEM EE-AH-OH-EH EH-LEE-ON

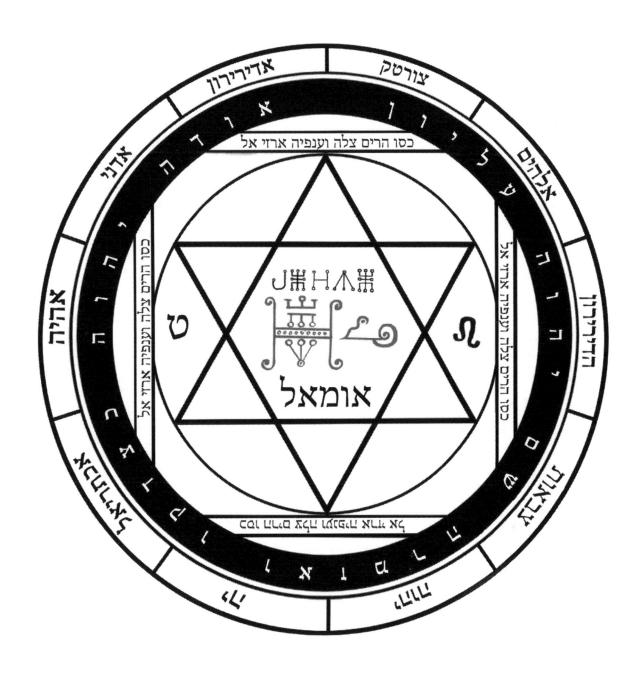

Omael

AWE-MUH-ELL

The Powers of Lecavel

Inspirational Ideas for Your Profession

Whatever work you do, you need good ideas to rise through the ranks, create new marketing opportunities or develop new products and directions for your work. When you want to improve your chances of promotion, or if you need a new product or a new way of marketing it to the world, or even ways to impress your boss or colleagues, call on this angel. The inspiration may come in bursts, or can manifest as a gradual awakening to new ideas.

Remain Unseen

There are times when you would rather not be seen. This angel cannot make you invisible, but it can make you inconspicuous. If you are going somewhere and would rather not be noticed, call on this angel. If you are being stalked or harassed, call on this angel to make you effectively invisible and uninteresting to your enemy. When you have received too much attention, call on the angel to find peace and to be left alone.

> Pronounced: LEK-AH-VELL
>
> Invocation (Psalm 31:14)
>
> VAH-AH-NEE AH-LECH-AH
> VAH-TAHCH-TEE
> EE-AH-OH-EH AH-MAHR-TEE
> ELL-AWE-HIGH AH-TAH

Lecavel

LEK-AH-VELL

The Powers of Vesheriah

The Power to Protect Against the Unfair

There may be people in your life who treat you unfairly, but it is not practical or desirable to move them out of your life. Whether this is somebody you love, or somebody you merely tolerate due to circumstances, you can call on this angel to protect you against the actions of the unfair person.

The Power to Empower Artists

If you are involved in the arts, this angel can empower your life. The angel will work to improve your skills, but will also work to ensure that you are in control of your artistic career, rather than being controlled by others. When you are seeking to network, form good business connections and get your work recognized, it is good to have this angel on your side to ensure that you remain in control of your creative work.

Pronounced: VESH-EH-REE-AH

Invocation (116:4)

OOV-SHEM
EE-AH-OH-EH
EK-RAH AH-NAH
EE-AH-OH-EH
MAH-LEH-TAH
NAHF-SHE

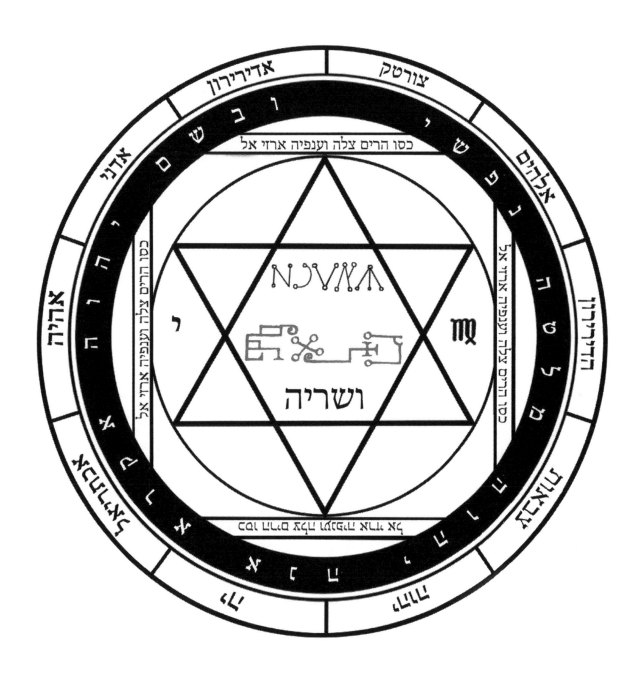

Vesheriah

VESH-EH-REE-AH

The Powers of Yichuiah

Destroy The Plans of an Enemy

When you know somebody is trying to bring harm to you, this is the angel to call. Whether you are going through a difficult divorce, being bullied at work, harassed in a relationship or attacked in business, this angel can help. The angel works best when you know your enemy and what they plan to do to you.

Make Superiors See the Truth

If you are falsely accused of something and you need your boss or other superior to know the truth, call on this angel. This angel can also be useful if you are accused of an offence you did not commit, and can help everybody to see your innocence.

Manifest Material Desires

If you have a strong material desire, this angel can help. If you covet something as simple as a new guitar, or even a new house, call on this angel. Don't aim for something that is too far out of reach, but focus on a desire that is strong, but that seems to be just a little too difficult to obtain right now. The angel can speed the manifestation up. If you are actively working other forms of magick to produce money or other material desires, use this angel to empower those workings and you will get stronger and faster results. This angel is also used by people who work in sales, to increase success.

Pronounced: YEE-CHOO-EE-AH

Invocation (Psalm 92:5)

MAH GAH-DEH-LOO
MAH-AH-SECH-AH
EE-AH-OH-EH MEH-AWED
AHM-EH-KOO
MAH-CHUH-SHEH-VAW-TECH-AH

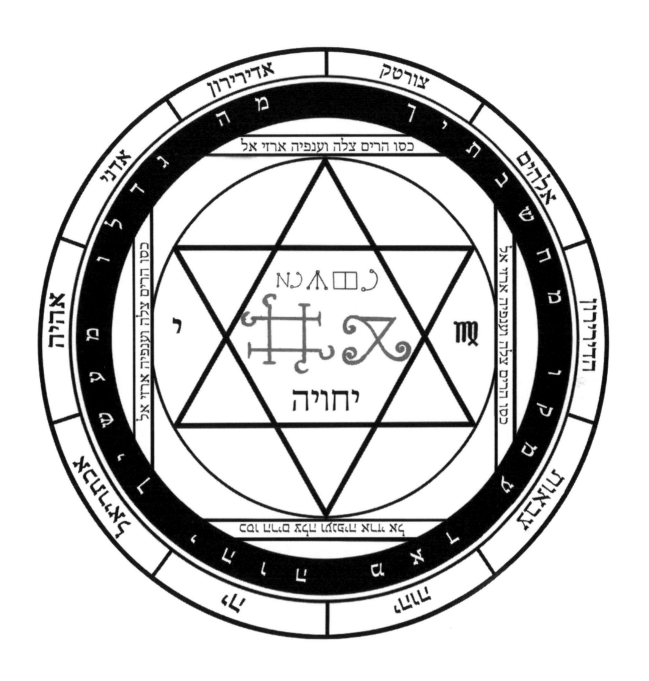

Yichuiah

YEE-CHOO-EE-AH

The Powers of Lehachiah

The Power to Halt Anger

When you have to spend time around an angry person, this angel can be called to reduce that person's anger. This is useful in difficult situations, such as a divorce, or when people are being pushed to extremes by difficult circumstances. It should not be seen as a cure for anger, however. If the person you are dealing with is naturally angry, this angel will only subdue them for a few weeks at a time. If you suffer from angry outbursts yourself, call on the angel to reduce your temper, and the results can last for many years.

The Power to Inspire Faithfulness

When you are concerned that your partner may be unfaithful, or is considering being unfaithful, this angel can remind them of their true feelings. If your partner still loves you, then temptation will be removed and the disloyalty will come to an end. If you are feeling a temptation to be disloyal, but still want to be faithful, you can call on the angel to inspire loyalty in yourself. This can help you resist temptation while you work on your relationship.

Pronounced: LEH-HAH-CHEE-AH

Invocation (Psalm 98:4)

HAH-REE-OO
LAH-EE-AH-OH-EH
KAWL HA-AH-RETZ
PEETZ-CHOO
VEH-RAH-NEH-NOO
VEH-SAH-MAY-ROO

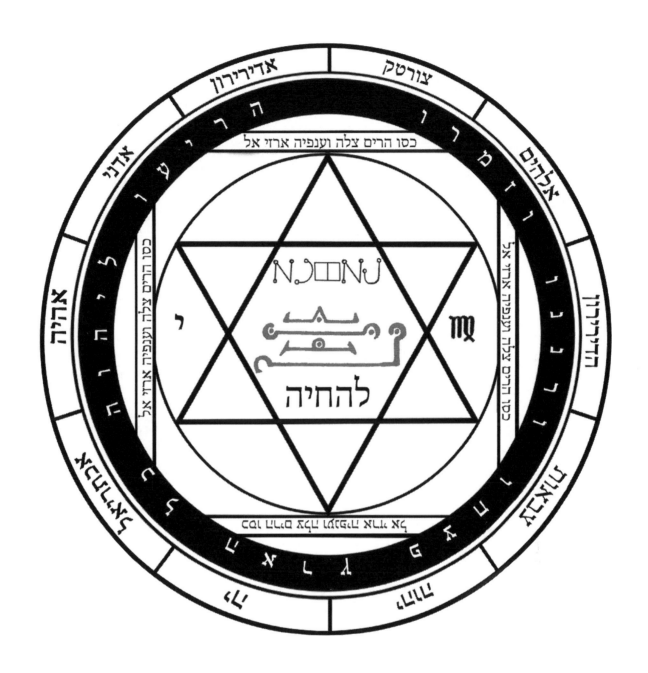

Lehachiah

LEH-HAH-CHEE-AH

The Powers of Kevekiah

The Power to Ensure a Good Inheritance

This angel can be called upon to ensure that you receive a good inheritance. This will not produce an inheritance out of the blue, but if you are expecting and entitled to an inheritance, it will ensure that you are given a generous share. Although this may seem like a greedy and selfish power, it is used by the wise to ensure that they are not tricked out of an inheritance. In many families there are people who try to get wills made out in their favor. This angel can prevent any injustice being done to you. It is best performed when you know a will is being prepared. If a will has already been prepared, you can still perform the magick and the angel can inspire a change to be made to the will.

The Power to Bring Peace to a Family

Families should be loving but are often at war. When these arguments get out of control, family members can estrange themselves and become enemies for life. Before it gets to that point, call on this angel to bring peace. If your family has already suffered great disruption, you can call on the angel to heal and reunite the family.

The Power to Ensure Friendly Sharing

When anything is being divided between a group of people, this angel can ensure that you get a generous share. This can be useful if somebody you know is planning to share wealth, winnings, property or anything else of value. Although these circumstances are rare, when they come about it is good to know that this angel will work miracles to ensure you are seen as a worthy recipient.

Pronounced: KEV-EK-EE-AH

Invocation (Psalm 88:13)

VAH-AH-NEE AIL-ECH-AH
EE-AH-OH-EH SHE-VAH-EH-TEA
OO-VAH-BAW-KER TEH-FEE-LAH-TEE
TEH-KAH-DEH-MEK-AH

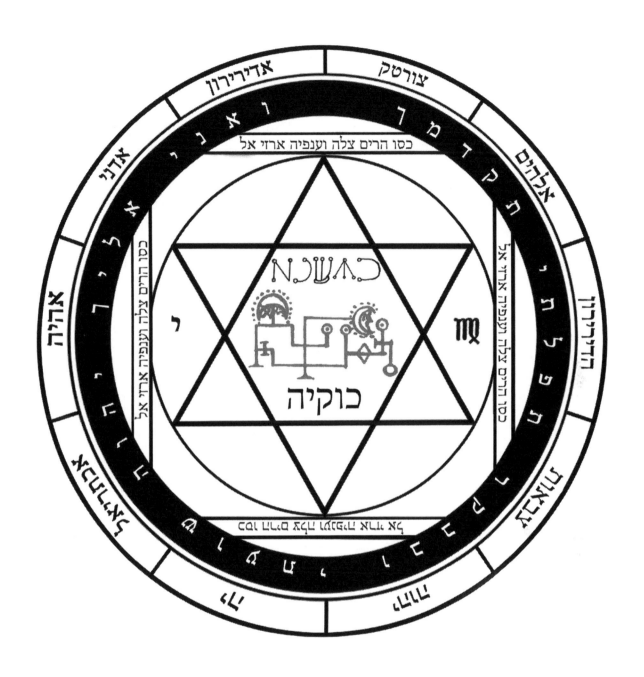

Kevekiah

KEV-EK-EE-AH

The Powers of Menadel

The Power to Keep a Job

Make sure you genuinely want to keep your job before calling on this angel. If your job is under threat, or if you are facing difficult circumstances, then job security is something you will crave. This power should not be used casually, though, because it may prevent you from being promoted or getting a better job. When you call on the angel, your request should make it clear that you want to keep your job for a set length of time. If you change your mind when another opportunity comes up, call the angel again, just once, and ask for the job protection to be removed. If the set length of time runs out, and you still fear for your job, you will need to repeat the ritual from another eleven days. An ideal way to work this is to ask the angel for a year of protection. That way, you can cancel the angel's power if there's a new opportunity, and you don't have to repeat the ritual too often.

The Power to Maintain a Career

This angel can help you to maintain your current level of career success. If you are afraid that your career could suffer, or that financial losses are around the corner, this angel can help you to get through difficult times. Be aware, however, that the angel will not encourage great growth in your career during this period of protection. As such, you should only use it when you fear there is a risk to your career. If new opportunities arise, and you see a potential for growth, you can cancel the protection by calling the angel once, and asking for the protection to be ceased.

Pronounced: MEN-AH-DELL

Invocation (Psalm 26:8)

EE-AH-OH-EH
AH-HAHV-TEE
MEH-AWN
BAIT-ECH-AH
OO-MEH-KAWM
MEESH-KAHN
KEH-VAW-DECH-AH

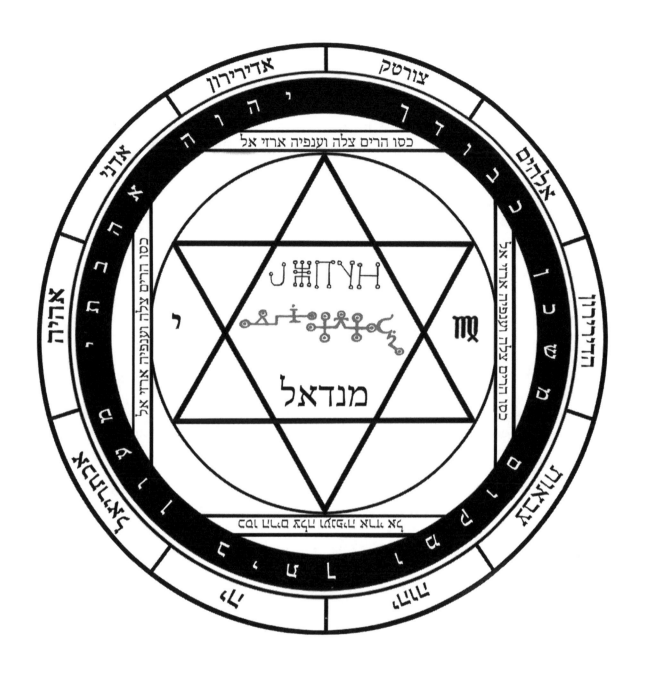

Menadel

MEN-AH-DELL

The Powers of Aniel

The Power to Create Good Fiction

There are many angels that help with good writing, but this angel is the one you call when you want to write good fiction. You can ask for a general improvement in your story-writing ability, or aim the magick at a specific project.

The Power to Create Art and Music

This angel gives you inspiration but also helps you find the opportunities that will enable your art to be shared and seen. This angel does not always ensure that you will make money from your increased popularity, but it will ensure that you work creatively and get your work seen. This is especially useful at an early point in your creative career.

The Power to Make Wise People Communicate

This sounds like quite an obscure power, but you may find there are occasions in your life when you need other people to communicate in order to get a result that suits you. Imagine, for example, that you are a writer and you want your agent to talk to a particular publisher. This angel could help to get the two parties talking. Although this seems like a power that may not be required often, it is one that I have used extensively and has helped me in many situations. Communication is the key to successful business, and yet even the wise will often shy away from communication with certain people. When you want a communication breakthrough, this is the power to call.

Pronounced: AH-KNEE-ELL

Invocation (Psalm 94:18)

EEM AH-MAHR-TEE
MAH-TAH RAH-GUH-LEE
HAHS-DEH-CHAH
EE-AH-OH-EH
YEES-AH-DAY-NEE

Aniel

AH-KNEE-ELL

The Powers of Chaamiah

The Power to Improve Wisdom

It's never a bad idea to improve your wisdom, but you may feel compelled to call on this angel if you are repeatedly making bad decisions. Chaamiah will help to make you think wisely and consider all options, so that you make fewer bad decisions. Some people only need to perform this ritual once in a lifetime to feel a significant change in their level of wisdom, but others repeat it every few years.

The Power to Improve Physical Health

When you are trying to improve your fitness or health, use this angel to support you. The angel will not increase your willpower, so it's up to you to put in the effort, but if you are dieting, exercising or working on any aspect of your health you can expect better results with the help of this angel.

Pronounced: CHAH-AH-ME-AH

Invocation (Psalm 91:9)

KEY AH-TAH
EE-AH-OH-EH
MAHCH-SEE
EH-LEE-AWN
SAHM-TAH
MEH-AWN-ECH-AH

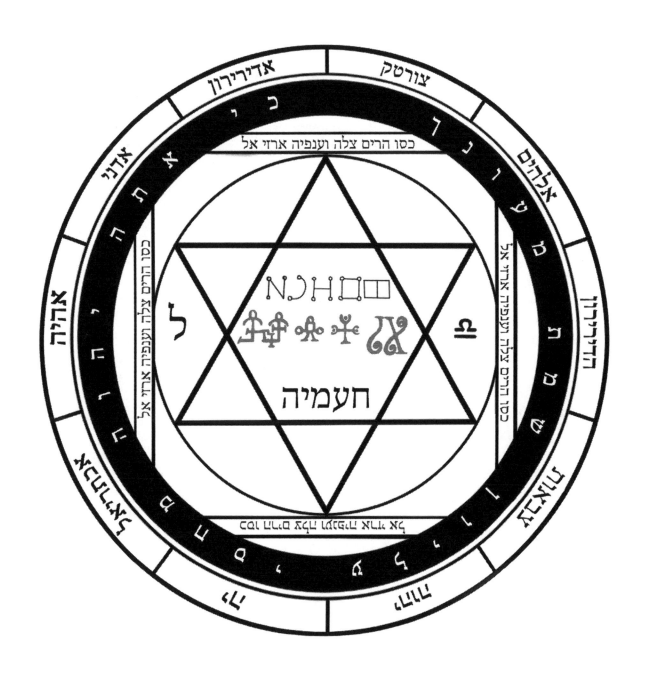

Chaamiah

CHAH-AH-ME-AH

The Powers of Rehoel

The Power to Cure an Illness

When an illness has come on suddenly, this angel can help you to recover more rapidly than usual. If you have the energy to perform this ritual for yourself, it will work well and will increase your energy levels, but you may find you use it more often for somebody else, because performing any magick when you are ill can be difficult. It works best on relatively minor and short-term illnesses, rather than life-threatening diseases.

The Power to Regenerate Energy

When you are exhausted or burnt out, it can be almost impossible to recover, because you never get the time or space to recover. This angel works in two ways. Firstly, it bends time so that you are able to get extra benefit from even short rest periods. Secondly, it will boost your energy levels, making recovery faster.

The Power to Obtain the Love of a Parent

There are many people who feel they are not loved by their parent. Often, this is a misperception, but in many cases it is the truth. If you feel that a parent judges you, looks down on you or sees you in a negative way, you can call on this angel's power. The angel will remind your parent of an extremely deep love, and you will notice rapid changes in your relationship.

Rehoel: REH-HAW-ELL

Invocation (Psalm 118:16)

YEH-MEEN EE-AH-OH-EH
RAW-MAY-MAH
YEH-MEEN EE-AH-OH-EH
AWE-SAH CHAH-EEL

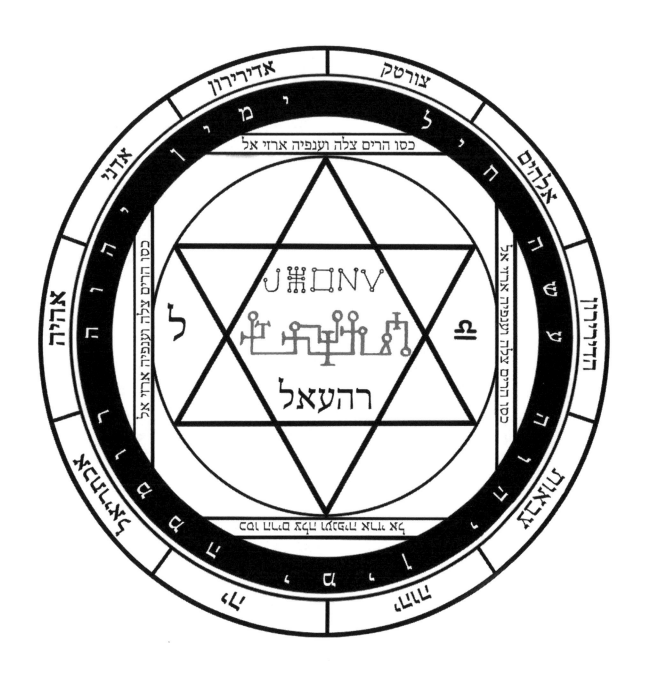

Rehoel

REH-HAW-ELL

The Powers of Yeyizel

The Power to Free Somebody from Enemies

This power is useful when you want to free another person from a situation where they are being bullied, persecuted or otherwise oppressed.

The Power to Improve Psychic Ability

Calling on this angel can help you to improve your overall intuition. If you are actively trying to enhance or develop psychic abilities, the angel will assist. If you are working with various magickal entities, and wish to make more direct contact, Yeyizel can help you become more aware of responses from other spirits.

The Power to Get Writing Published

There are many places to get your writing published in the modern world, without having to go through the 'gatekeepers' of the publishing industry, but many people would like to see their work published by a famous newspaper or book publisher. If you write for this sort of market, this angel can help open that pathway to publication.

Pronounced: YAY-EEZ-ELL

Invocation (Psalm 115:11)

YEAR-EH EE-AH-OH-EH
BEE-TUH-CHOO
VAH-EE-AH-OH-EH
EZRAHM
OOM-AH-GEE-NAHM WHO

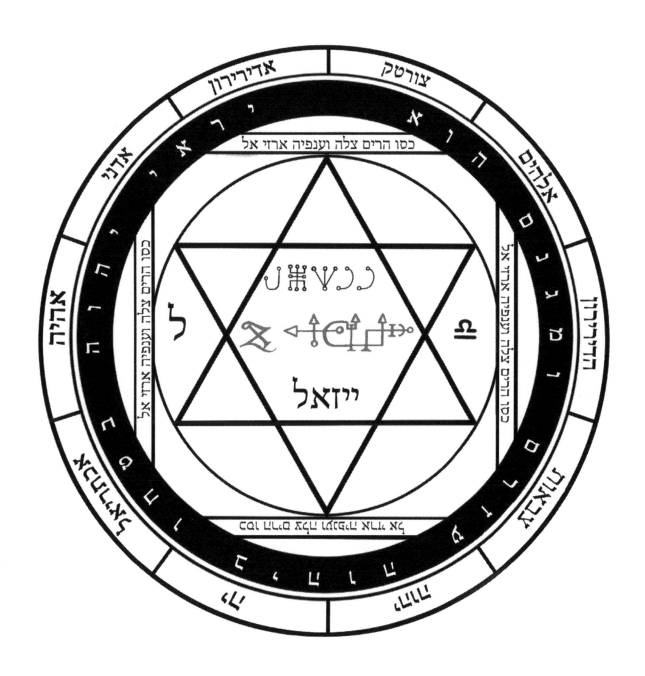

Yeyizel

YAY-EEZ-ELL

The Powers of Hahahel

The Power to Stop Enemies

This power is used not only to stop enemies from harming you, but from having power over others. When you want to bring a cruel person to a halt, and prevent them from bullying and harassing yourself and others, this angel will make that person lack the strength of will to attack.

The Power to Strengthen Inner Nature

If you find that you feel distant from yourself, or that you lack inner strength, or feel ashamed of who you are, call on this angel. You will gain more self-esteem, more self-respect and the strength to express your personality without a sense of shame.

Pronounced: HAH-AH-ELL

Invocation (Psalm 120:2)

EE-AH-OH-EH
HAH-TSEEL-AH NAHF-SHE
MEES-FAHT SHEK-ERR
MEEL-ASH-AWN
REH-MEE-AH

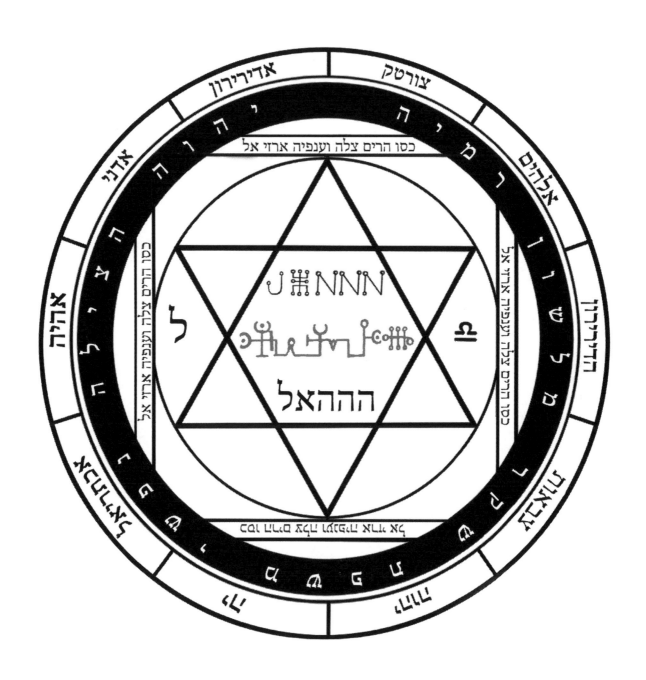

Hahahel

HAH-AH-ELL

The Powers of Michel

The Power to Help Politicians

If you work in politics, you can call on this angel for help with any aspect of your work. This angel can also be used by a politician's supporters and campaigners, to increase popularity or get a message across.

The Power to Influence Politicians

When you need a politician on your side, or want to change a politician's opinion to aid your cause, call on this angel. You are unlikely to change a politician's core beliefs, but you can make them more open-minded about subjects that matter to you.

The Power to Influence the Powerful

This angel will give you the power to influence the thoughts, feelings and decisions of anybody who has more power than you in a given situation. The key word here is 'influence'. You are not taking complete control of another person's will, but influencing their thoughts and feelings to bend their decisions in the direction of your choosing.

Pronounced: ME-CHUH-ELL

Invocation (Psalm 121:7)

EE-AH-OH-EH
YEESH-MORE-CHAH
MEEK-AWL RAH
YEESH-MORE ET
NAHF-SHECH-AH

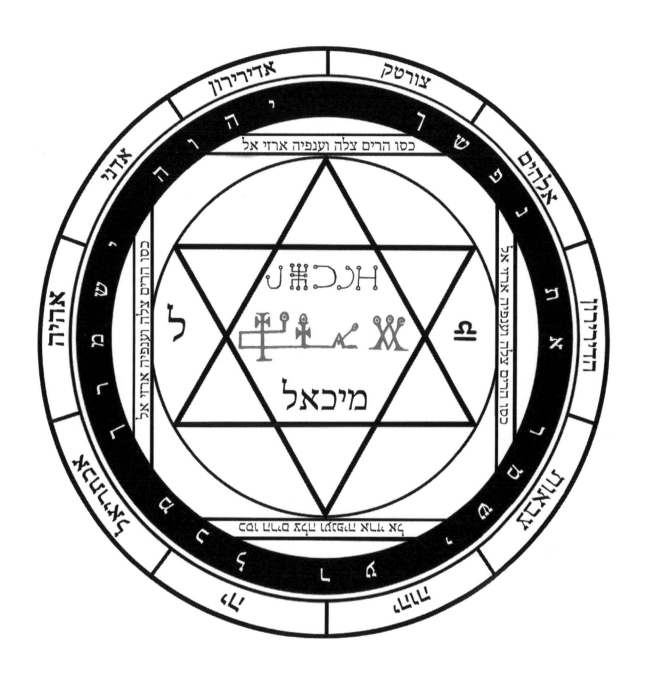

Michel

ME-CHUH-ELL

The Powers of Vevaliah

Destroy Enemies

When you are bullied, subjugated, persecuted or harmed by an enemy that will not give up, you want to destroy your enemy. This angel can be used to curse your enemies and bring harm to them, such as bad luck or ill health. The angel can be used to bind them and keep them quiet. If you want a subtler approach you can destroy your enemy's ability to harm you or their ability to work or think effectively. When calling on this angel, remember the pain your enemy has brought to you as clearly as you can.

Punish a Cruel Superior

If you are being bothered or bullied by somebody who ranks higher than you, in your organization or in life, call on this angel to subdue and punish that person. The 'superior' may be an employer, somebody in your company, a personal you deal with, or even a friend or neighbor who acts as though they are superior. This angel will punish the person by bringing harm and discomfort if you ask for that, but you can simply ask that the person stops being cruel and feels terrible guilt and remorse.

Develop a Reputation of Power

Bullying happens all the time in all kinds of relationships, from the most personal to the professional. It can happen online, in person and sometimes so subtly that you don't even realize the harm that's being done. To avoid people trying to bully you or take advantage of you, develop a reputation of power. This enables you to be seen as a good, friendly and strong person, without having to look angry or aggressive. In many situations, this reputation of power and control is the best possible approach to protecting yourself and projecting yourself to greater success.

Pronounced: VEH-VAH-LEE-AH

Invocation (Psalm 121:8)

EE-AH-OH-EH YEESH-MORE
TZAY-TEH-CHAH
OO-VAW-ECHAH
MAY-AH-TAH VEH-AHD AWE-LAHM

Vevaliah

VEH-VAH-LEE-AH

The Powers of Yelahiah

The Power to Ease the Mind

At the end of a long project, or when you have worried about something for a long time, this angel can ease your mental anguish. This angel is also useful for reducing anxiety in social situations, and can be used by people who suffer from social anxiety to obtain a calm confidence.

The Power to Manifest Objects

If there is a material object you desire greatly, you can call on this angel to lead you to that object. If you are looking to buy a car, the angel will guide you to the best possible car at the best price. If you want a house, in a good area, you will be guided to find the best house. You will still have to pay for these material objects (so be grateful there is plenty of money magick in the world), but this remains an extremely effective power. When you are seeking to manifest something physical with the best conditions for the fairest price, this angel brings fast results.

The Power to Improve Business Matters

When your business needs to change for the better, call on this angel for guidance, and to support the efforts you make to improve your business. The angel is particularly effective at getting you a better deal, a better price or better conditions when dealing with others.

Pronounced: YELL-AH-EE-AH

Invocation (Psalm 106:2)

MEE YEH-MAH-LAY
GUH-VOO-RAWT
EE-AH-OH-EH YAH-SHMEE-AH
KAWL TEH-HEEL-AH-TAW

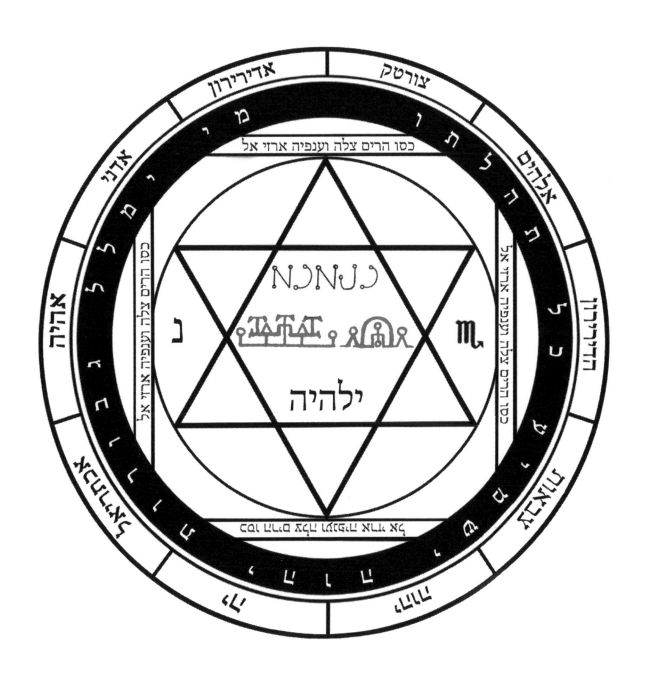

Yelahiah

YELL-AH-EE-AH

The Powers of Sealiah

The Power to Uncover a Curse

If you suspect that you have been cursed, this angel will reveal details of the curse, while rendering the curse ineffective. At the same time, the person who has cursed you will become aware of your power and afraid to curse you again. You will feel the curse begin to lift soon after starting the ritual, and then you will experience moments of intuition and fragments of dream that let you know where the curse came from.

The Power to Recover Your Rights

If you feel that your rights have been taken away from you, in any situation, this angel can get them back for you. This works in legal situations, but even in areas such as the 'rights' you have within your family or at work.

The Power to Improve Education

This angel will find ways to give you access to better education, and make you more receptive to learning. If you need to develop yourself and your education, before taking the next step in your career, call on this angel. If you want more education, but are uncertain of what form of study suits you, this angel can guide you to choose the right subject, course and even the best place to study.

Pronounced: SEH-AH-LEE-AH

Invocation (Psalm 33:22)

YEH-HE HAHS-DEH-CHAH
EE-AH-OH-EH AH-LAY-NOO
KAH-AH-SHER
YEE-CHAHL-NOO LAHCH

Sealiah

SEH-AH-LEE-AH

The Powers of Ariel

Discover Hidden Treasure

When you need extra money, call on this angel to bring money from unexpected sources. You may find that you are owed money, or you get refunds, or that some other source provides money from out of the blue. This approach is best when you want a surprise boost of cash, rather than a huge shift in your earnings. If you are somebody who works in an industry where you actually seek out treasure – such as the antiques trade, mining or exploration - then the angel can work absolute miracles.

Learn About Desires Through Dreams

If you aren't certain what you want, it's a terrible thing. When you see an actor, business owner or politician working with single-minded determination, it feels terrible if *you* aren't sure what *you* want. The truth may be that you only want a simple life, or a little more money, but your desires may be more daring. If you're ever uncertain of your path, call on the wisdom of this angel to open your eyes to your true desires.

Planning with a Strong and Subtle Mind

Before you begin a major project of any kind – from asking somebody out on a date, to taking over another company - you need to plan with a subtle mind. When you are faced with a major challenge, call on this angel to give you the time and space to plan quietly and discreetly. You will be granted the power to make plans without anybody perceiving your plans, making them all the more powerful.

Pronounced: AH-REE-ELL

Invocation (Psalm 38:21)

AHL TAH-AHZ-VAY-NEE
EE-AH-OH-EH
ELL-AWE-HIGH
AL TEER-CHAHK
MEEM-EN-EE

Ariel

AH-REE-ELL

The Powers of Eshaliah

The Power to Create Love

While some angels can open hearts and expand love, this angel can create love where there is none. This does not work if you are merely attracted to somebody, but if you love somebody and they do not love you in return, this angel can stir feelings in their heart. This angel can also be used in a relationship where you feel that the other person is afraid of loving you or unwilling to make a commitment. This angel will not pull anybody away from their true will, but will gladly generate new feelings to assist in your loving ventures, so long as your feelings are completely sincere.

The Power to See the Past, Present and Future

You can call on this angel to uncover lost memories, to see the present more clearly and to get an idea of what is coming in the future. Your requests can be general or extremely specific and limited to a particular subject. You may see a series of signs or omens that hint at the future, but you should also experience brief flashes of memory, images of the future and a growing sense of your current reality. Many answers will come to you in dreams.

The Power to Discover More About Your Self

Some of the greatest powers in this book are the ones that can be overlooked. It's easy to spend decades in the wrong career, with the wrong partner, doing things that make you unhappy, because momentum carries you along and denies you self-knowledge.

Calling on this angel will give you a deep insight into who you really are and what you really want. The discoveries may be quite a revelation, so be prepared to experience transformation.

Pronounced: ESH-AH-LEE-AH

Invocation (Psalm 100:2)

EAVE-DO ET EE-AH-OH-EH
BEH-SEEM-CHAH
BAW-OO LEH-FAH-NAHV
BEER-NAHN-AH

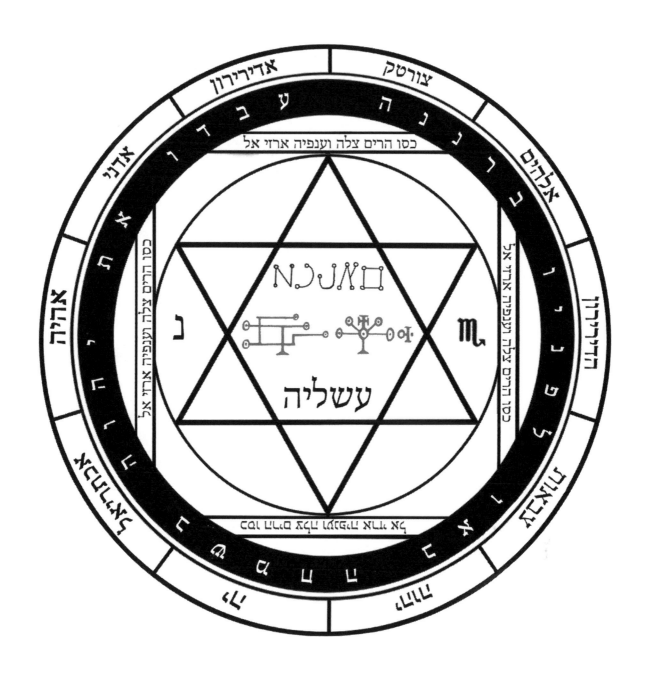

Eshaliah

ESH-AH-LEE-AH

The Powers of Mihel

The Power to Create Peace in a Marriage

Marriages, or other long-term relationships, can easily fall into patterns of bickering, blaming and arguing that conceal genuine love. This angel will remove the petty barriers that create friction in your relationship, and let you both experience love. The angel can even help when a relationship has become filled with spite and anger.

The Power to Excite Physical Love

When there is already some love present in a relationship, this angel can help to take things to a much more exciting physical level. It can bring more pleasure to both parties. If you want increased passion and sensuality, this angel will help introduce a heartfelt lust that gives you the opportunity to express your love physically.

Mihel is pronounced: ME-HUH-ELL

Invocation (Psalm 109:30)

AWE-DEH EE-AH-OH-EH
MEH-AWED BEH-FEE
OO-VUH-TAWCH
RAH-BEEM AH-HAH-LEH-LEN-OO

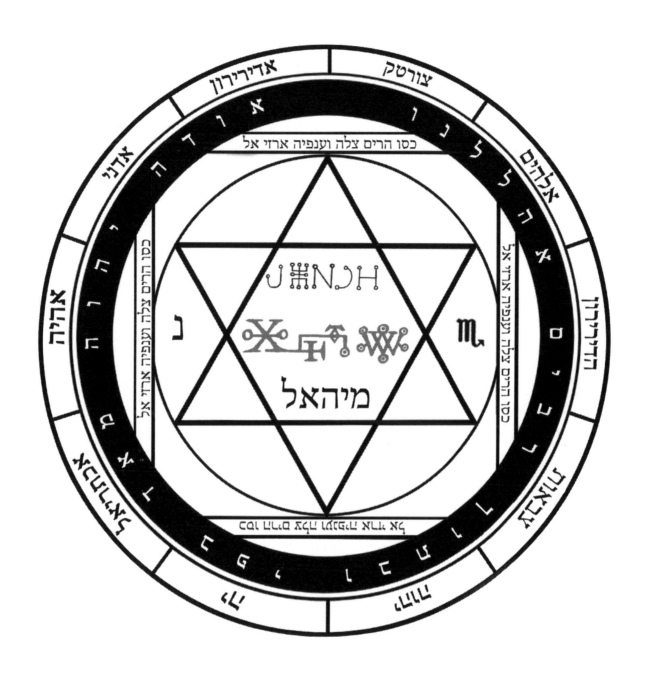

Mihel

ME-HUH-ELL

The Powers of Vehuel

The Power to Know Another's Thoughts
When you want to know what somebody thinks about a particular situation, this angel can help you to know their thoughts. This works when you know the person in question and see them on a regular basis. The angel gives you the power to see through their words and sense the truth behind their words. You may also get flashes of insight into their deeper thoughts and feelings on the subject.

The Power to Calm an Aggressive Situation
This angel works most effectively when aimed at one specific aggressive situation. If, for example, you have an ongoing problem with an aggressive neighbor, the angel will subdue that person. If there is one house on your street that attracts trouble and lawlessness, the angel can remove those people from your life or calm them down. Wherever you experience regular aggression, the angel can bring calm.

The Power to Make Somebody Humble
If you live or work with somebody who has a huge ego, it can affect your mood and the quality of your work and relationship. This angel can make an egotistical person humble.

The Power to Dominate Strong Personalities
Strong personalities are a good thing, and if you want to thrive in life you will probably need to be surrounded by people with strong personalities at times. There will be occasions, though, where you need to influence these people, and influencing somebody who is very sure of themselves can be difficult. Call on this angel to give you the power to dominate somebody with a strong personality, so that they hear you, respond to you and are willing to let you take the lead in a situation.

Pronounced: VEH-WHO-ELL

Invocation (Psalm 145:3)

GAH-DAWL EE-AH-OH-EH
OO-MEH-HOO-LAHL
MEH-AWED
VEH-LEE-GUH-DOO-LAH-TOE
AIN CHAI-KERR

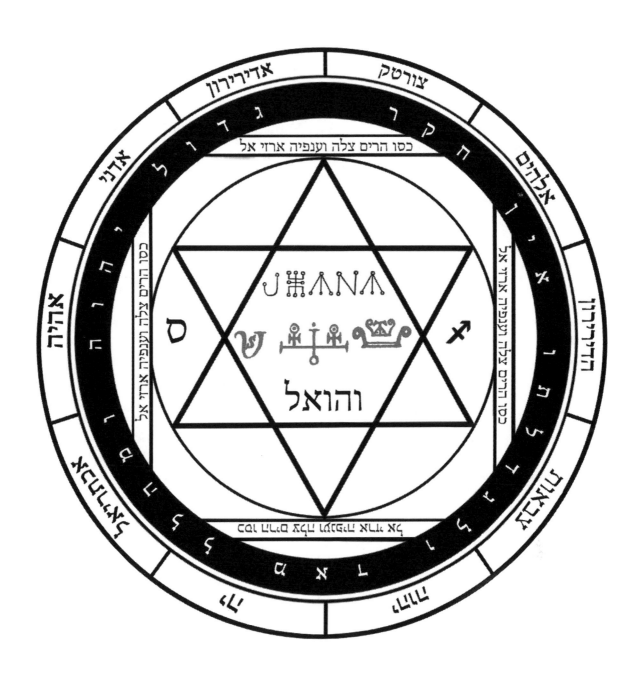

Vehuel

VEH-WHO-ELL

The Powers of Daniel

Help with Legal Decisions
When you need a legal decision to fall in your favor, call on this angel. If you can name the judge, or other person of power, that will help, but it is not an absolute requirement. This angel can also help you to be wise when making a legal decision. If you are about to respond to a legal action, or take legal action yourself, call on this angel to give you the wisdom and clarity you desire.

To Help a Good Decision to be Made
You think you know what you want, but how often do you find yourself saying, 'I just don't know what to do'? I hear this all the time, from friends, relations and readers of my books. People state the problem, but then make it absolutely clear they don't know what solution they want. If the marriage has failed, should they leave or try to mend it? If business is bad should they start again, or work with what they have? When you feel too muddled, confused or influenced by others to think straight, call on this angel for clarity. You will find your thoughts become sharp, your emotions will be under control and you will make the best possible decision.

To Write Well
These days, everybody writes. Whether you're writing an email, a poem, a novel or a business plan, you are more likely to get good results if you write well. When your writing matters, call on this angel to help. If you write often, you can work with this angel and ask to be helped with your writing for many years, or you can target the magick to a specific project if that matters more at the time.

To Get a Message Out to the World
This is the angel of publicity. When you want to get a message out to the world, especially a written message, call on this angel. Whether you are looking to make a blog post popular, get an important letter read by the right person or get your book published, this angel can help get your message out to the world.

Pronounced: DAH-NEE-ELL

Invocation (Psalm 9:1)

AWE-DEH EE-AH-OH-EH BUH-CHAWL
LEE-BEE AH-SAH-PEH-RAH
KAWL NEEF-LEH-AWE-TECH-AH

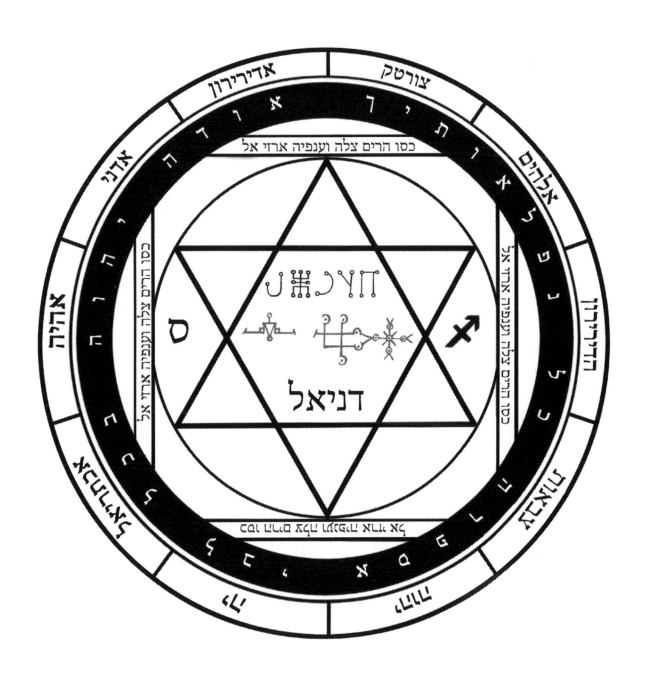

Daniel

DAH-NEE-ELL

The Powers of Hachashiah

The Power to Handle Complex Projects

When you take on a complex project, there is a risk of being overwhelmed. Call on this angel to give you the confidence and clarity of mind to handle a situation that challenges you. The greatest power of this angel is to help you hold the whole project in your mind clearly. This is why it is useful to novelists, architects, managers, wedding planners or anybody who needs to remember a thousand details at one time. If you are ever faced with a task that seems more complex than you can handle, trust that this angel will help you through to the end.

The Power to Improve Clarity of Thought

Whatever you are working on, this angel can help bring greater clarity to your thoughts. If you find that you are feeling muddled, confused or overwhelmed, this angel will help you see the whole situation so that you can make better judgments about how to make decisions.

Pronounced: HAH-CHAH-SHE-AH

Invocation (Psalm 104:31)

YEH-HE CHEH-VAWED
EE-AH-OH-EH LEH-AWE-LAHM
YEESH-MAHCH EE-AH-OH-EH
BEH-MAH-AH-SAHV

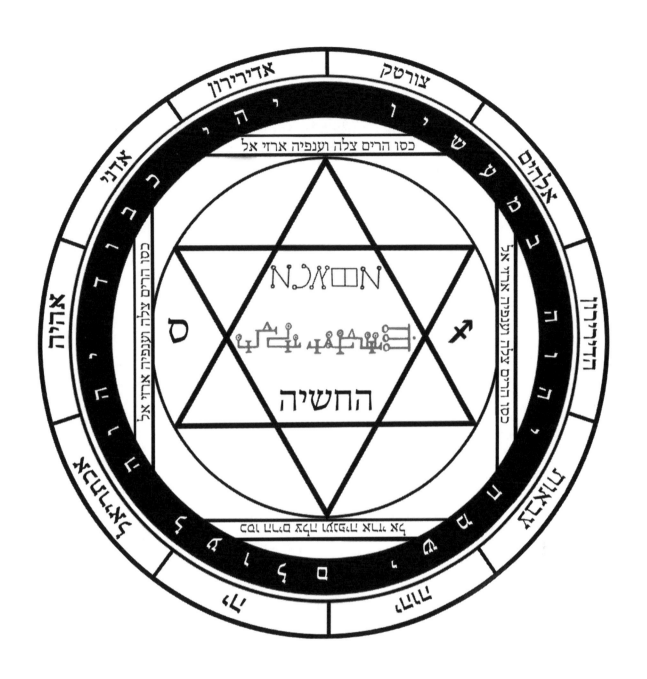

Hachashiah

HAH-CHAH-SHE-YAH

The Powers of Omemiah

The Power to Weaken an Enemy

When you know that you are being attacked by somebody, directly or subtly, this angel will gladly weaken your enemy. Some angels can stop an enemy in their tracks, so why would you want to weaken an enemy? Sometimes, it is better if other people witness you getting the better of an enemy. If you are being bullied in the workplace and the bully just leaves, people may think of you as weak (even though the bullying was never your problem). If you weaken your enemy, people will see that you have overcome the obstacle and will respect you more. The other time to use this angel is when you are being attacked by a particularly vicious or fearsome enemy – use this angel to first weaken your enemy, and then use other angels to bring about the enemy's defeat.

The Power to Research Well

We have so much access to information that it is difficult to research well. To learn a new skill, to understand your business or to develop your career, you need to research constantly. Call on this angel to give you the power to research well, and your research abilities will be more focused and creative for many years.

Pronounced: AWE-MEM-EE-AH

Invocation (Psalm 25:6)

ZEH-CHOAR RAH-CHAH-MECH-AH
EE-AH-OH-EH
VAH-CHAH-SAH-DEH-CHAH
KEY MAY-AWE-LAHM
HAY-MAH

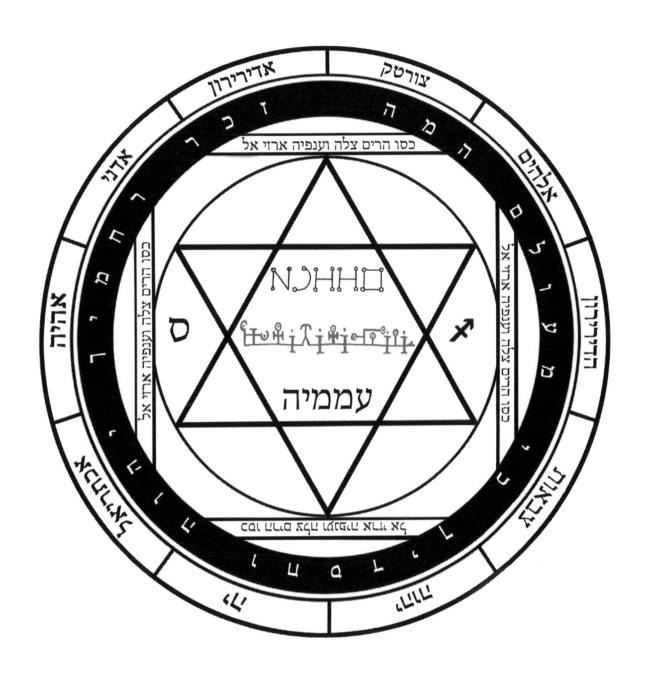

Omemiah

AWE-MEM-EE-AH

The Powers of Nenael

To Improve Your Skills

When you are working on your skills, in any area, from sport to public speaking, this angel will help. Even if this is an area where you have little or no natural talent, your skills can be improved. I've seen this angel used by musicians, accountants and even politicians.

To Teach What You Have Learned

If you ever want to pass on your skills to another, call on this angel. The angel is also of great assistance to all who teach, making your work clear and your students attentive.

Pronounced: NEN-AH-ELL

Invocation (Psalm 33:18)

HEE-NAY AIN
EE-AH-OH-EH
EL YEH-RUH-AHV
LAH-ME-AH-CHAH-LEEM
LEH-CHAHS-DAW

Nenael

NEN-AH-ELL

The Powers of Nitel

The Power to Bring Stability

When there is chaos in any area of your life, this angel can bring stability. You can even use this angel in advance, when you suspect that a coming situation may be chaotic, to ensure that it remains stable.

The Power to Bring Fame to Artists and Writers

This angel can help to bring recognition to your artistic work, even in the early stages of your career. When you put your work out there, call on this angel to assist you in being found, recognized and appreciated.

Pronounced: NEAT-UH-ELL

Invocation (Psalm 16:5)

EE-AH-OH-EH MEH-NAHT
CHEL-KEY
VEH-CHAWE-SEE
AH-TAH
TAWE-MEECH
GAW-RAH-LEE

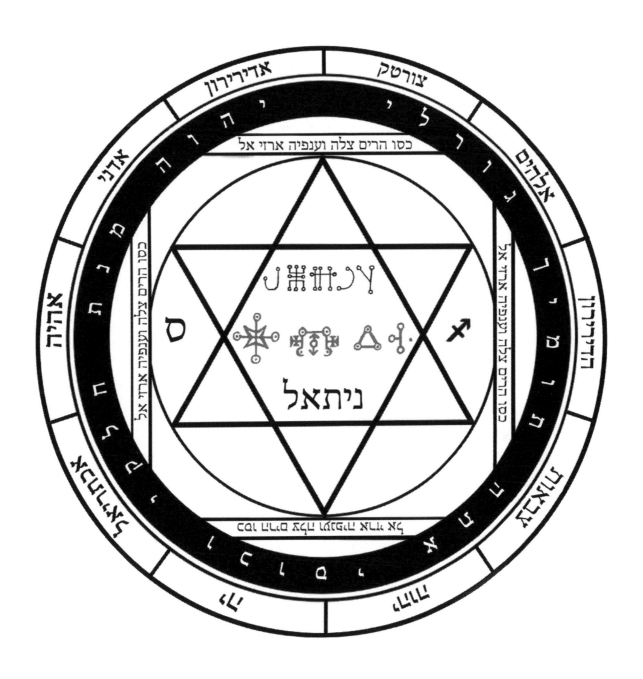

Nitel

NEAT-UH-ELL

The Powers of Mivahiah

The Power to Win Awards

This angel will not help you win the lottery or other games of chance, but if you are ever trying to win an award on merit, this angel can have astonishing results. I have seen this angel used by poets, filmmakers, artists, and singers to ensure that they get nominated for awards and then go on to win them.

The Power to Help Another

All the angelic powers in this book can be used to help others, but this power enables you to offer a gift to somebody you love or care about. It is not used to solve problems, but to give that person something that will make them happier. Leave it to the angel to decide what that person will receive. This power is useful when you feel that you owe a debt to somebody but have no way to pay them directly.

Pronounced: ME-VAH-EE-AH

Invocation (Psalm 103:19)

EE-AH-OH-EH
BAH-SHAH-MY-EEM
HAY-CHEEN KEES-AWE
OOM-AHL-CHOO-TAW
BAH-KAWL MAH-SHAH-LAH

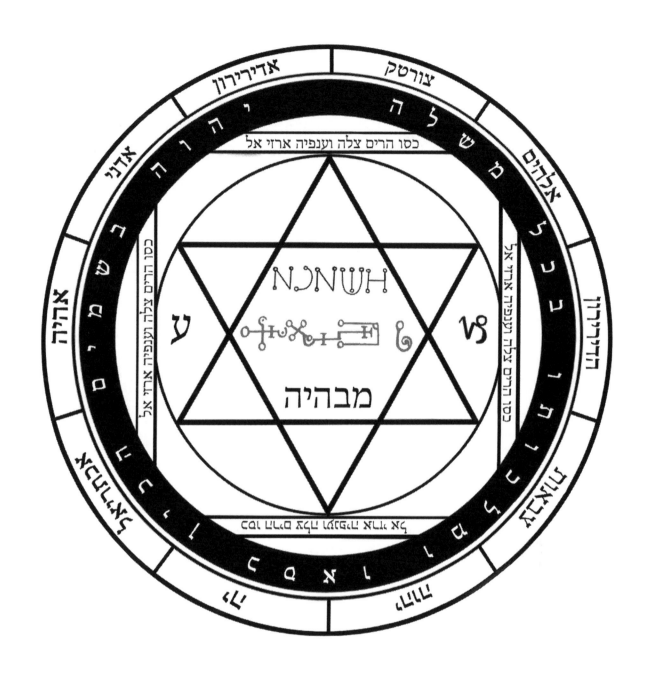

Mivahiah

ME-VAH-HEE-AH

The Powers of Poiel

To Obtain Any Desire

This power sounds a little too good to be true, but it is one that the members of The Gallery of Magick have all used with good results. Make sure you call on this angel when the desire seems vital to your very existence, rather than merely because the desire is pleasing to you. Ask for help when you have a desire that seems to suit your life, but currently seems impossible or out of reach. A second approach is to use this magick when you have a desire that has almost come to fruition several times, but has never quite made it through to reality. This angel will break through the barrier.

To Increase Fame and Fortune

This angel can help to build your personal charisma, and also develops your fame and your luck. To get the best results, ask for an increase in fame and fortune in a particular area of your life that matters greatly to you. Ideally, this should be your main profession, or a hobby that you want to turn into a profession. In short, use the power on things that really matter to you, and that have the potential to bring fame and fortune.

To Bring Fame Through Talent

When you are working with your natural talent, this angel can help to make you famous through the application of your talent. Call on the angel to make your talent become recognized by those who can help you. Ask the angel to bring you fame where it matters most, and to make your fans love you for the genuine talent you are offering. When promoting yourself in any way, you will need to market aspects of yourself that are not related to your talent, but this angel works to make your talent be seen most clearly. If you are a performer, the angel will ensure that your performances succeed and make you more famous.

Pronounced: PAW-EE-ELL

Invocation (Psalm 149:4)

KEY RAW-TSAY EE-AH-OH-EH
BEH-AH-MAW YEH-FAH-AIR
AH-NAH-VEEM BEE-SHOO-AH

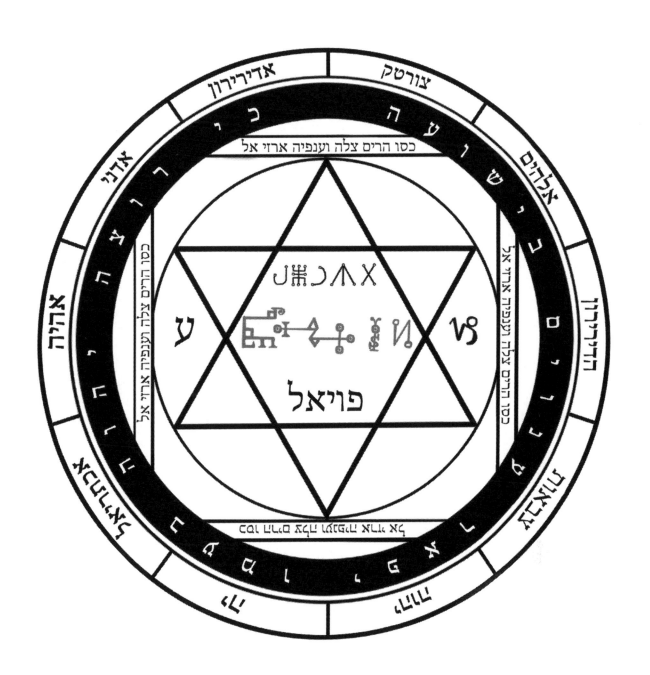

Poiel

PAW-EE-ELL

The Powers of Nememiah

The Power to Improve Prosperity

When your earnings start to increase, call on this angel to keep up your financial momentum. This is not an angel to call on when you are in poverty, but when you find that your circumstances have started to improve, this angel will ensure that money flows into your life to create a steady improvement in your overall prosperity.

The Power to Ease Anxiety

Many angels can ease the mind, but this angel works best when there is a particular concern that is making you anxious. If you are worried about an upcoming audition, interview, public appearance or any other occasion, call on this angel. If you don't have time to complete the ritual before the occasion in question, that doesn't matter – begin the ritual on a Thursday and you will feel your anxiety ease immediately. If the event passes before you have completed eleven days, make sure you continue with the ritual to the final Sunday even when the event has passed, but instead of making a request simply thank the angel.

Pronounced: NEM-EM-EE-AH

Invocation (Psalm 145:14)

SAW-MAYCH EE-AH-OH-EH
LEH-CHAWL
HAH-NAW-FEH-LEEM
VEH-ZAW-KAYF
LEH-CHAWL
HAH-KEH-FOO-FEEM

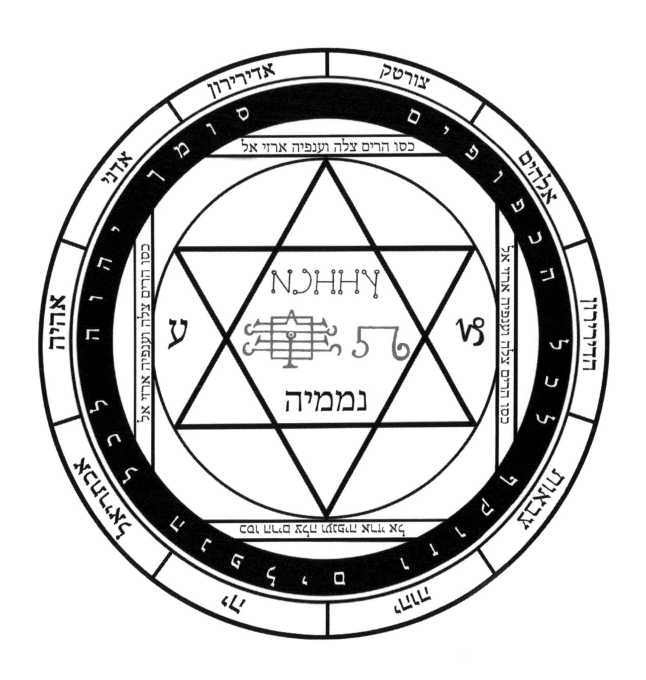

Nememiah

NEM-EM-EE-AH

The Powers of Yeyilel

The Power to Heal Sorrow

When you have an emotional pain that lingers, especially if it is caused by the loss of a loved one, this angel can heal your sorrow. If you suffer from regret, this angel can help you to move on and focus on the present and the future.

The Power to Work with Metal

This is quite an obscure power that may not be of use to most readers, but this angel is loved by those who trade in metal ores, or anybody who crafts metallic jewelry. The angel is able to ensure you obtain metals at good prices, and for those who work directly with metal it ensures that your work is skillful. The angel has been used by mechanics to improve their metal working skills.

Pronounced: YEH-YEE-LUH-ELL

Invocation (Psalm 113:2)

YEH-HE SHEM EE-AH-OH-EH
MEH-VAW-RAHCH
MAY-AH-TAH
VAY-AHD AWE-LAHM

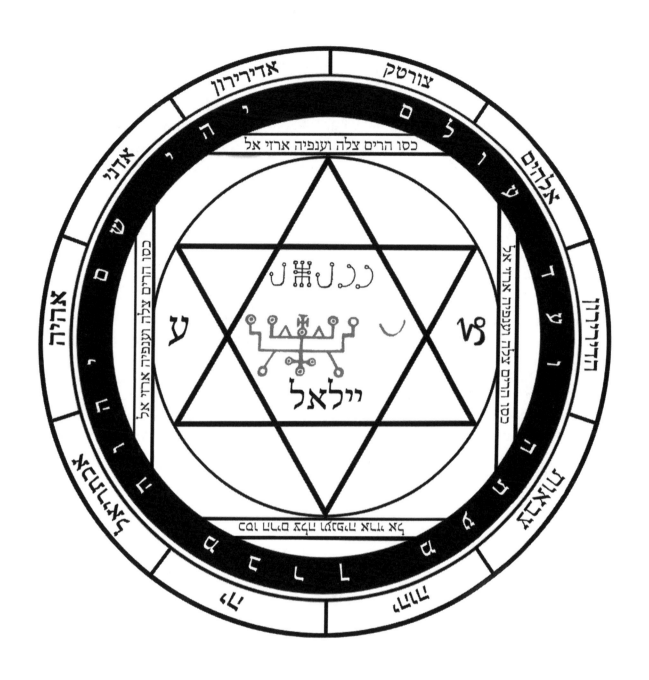

Yeyilel

YEH-YEE-LUH-ELL

The Powers of Harachel

The Power to Improve Fertility

Health magick of any kind runs the risk of offering false hope, but many angels have been employed to assist with fertility for countless years. As with all things medical, you should seek conventional help before turning to magick, but if you want to add magickal power to your efforts, this is the angel to call.

The Power to Influence Business People

There are many reasons you may wish to influence somebody who works in business. If you work in business, there are competitors and allies you could influence. Your living space may be affected by noise or other disruptions from a local business, and the best way to influence somebody to change their ways may be with magick. There are countless creative ways to use this power, to make more money or just make the peace.

The Power to Influence the Press

Whether you a trying to hide a story, get facts corrected, or get the press to give you some publicity, the ability to influence the press should never be underestimated. In the modern world, the press refers to blogs, websites and all other spaces where professionals write – as well as traditional print newspapers. This angel works best when you are trying to influence professional writers, rather than amateurs.

Pronounced: HAH-RAH-CHELL

Invocation (Psalm 94:22)

VEYE-HE EE-AH-OH-EH
LEE LUH-MEES-GAHV
VAY-LAW-HIGH
LUH-TZOOR
MAHCH-SEE

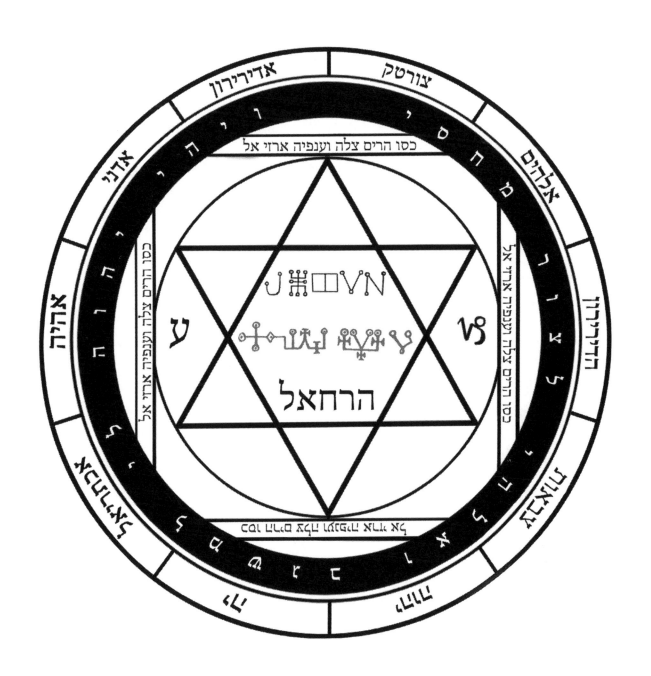

Harachel

HAH-RAH-CHELL

The Powers of Metzerel

The Power to be Free of Bullies

It's often difficult to tell when you are being bullied, and at other times it is obvious. If you feel that somebody is treating you unfairly and trying to control you, through threats, insults or subtler bullying, this angel can free you from that bully. Be aware that this angel tends to remove bullies from your life, so if you simply want to subdue or calm a bully you may want to call on a different angel. Metzerel will find ways to get bullies to move away from you, so they are no longer a concern.

The Power to Heal an Uneasy Spirit

If you find yourself feeling anxious for no obvious reason, or disappointed when things are going well, you can call on this angel to lift your spirit. If a coming task seems overwhelming, this angel can also help to prepare you for what's ahead.

The Power to Improve Your Loyalty to Another

Even in good relationships it may happen that you meet somebody who stirs your interest, and tempts you away from your current partner. This angel will help to keep you focused on the love you have for your current partner.

Pronounced: MET-ZEH-RELL

Invocation (Psalm 34:16)

PEH-NAY EE-AH-OH-EH
BEH-AWE-SAY RAH
LEH-HAHCH-REET
MAY-EH-RETZ
ZEECH-RAHM

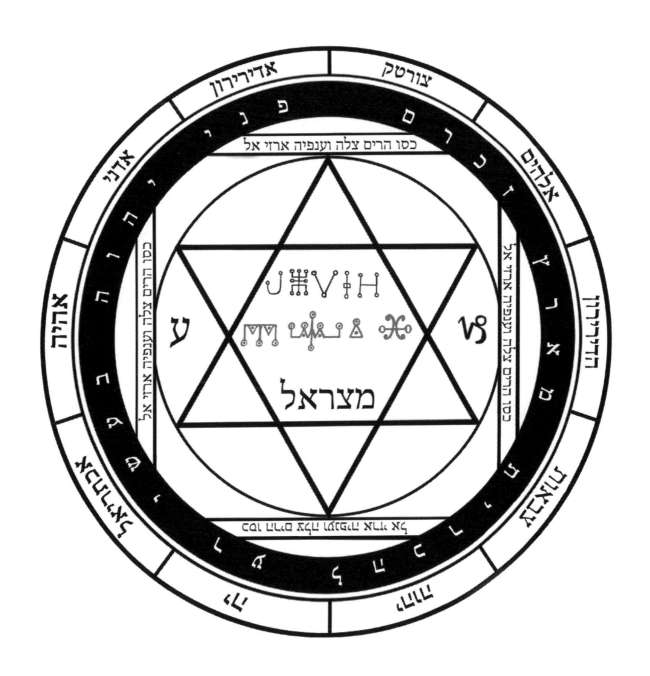

Metzerel

MET-ZEH-RELL

The Powers of Umabel

To Obtain Friendship

If you want more friends, call on this angel to attract people who can become genuine and worthwhile friends. If there is somebody you like, but that person has never really warmed to you, this angel can help to open up the friendship between you.

To Calm Passion into Friendship

If somebody has fallen in love with you and you want to be friends, call on this angel to calm the passion without hurting the other person. This will enable you to be friends without any risk of the passion getting in the way. You can also call on this angel to help you resist passion. If you are in a committed relationship and find yourself deeply attracted to somebody but want to remain faithful, this angel will help you turn the passion to something calmer.

Be Popular at Work

Call on this angel to get your co-workers, and even your boss, to like you. Be wary of being too popular, because sometimes the 'nice guy' seems too friendly to be hungry enough to rise to the top. If you are the boss, this is a fantastic angel to get your workers to like you.

Pronounced: OOM-AB-ELL

Invocation (Psalm 8:9)

EE-AH-OH-EH
AH-DAW-NAY-NOO
MAH AH-DEER
SHE-MUH-CHAH
BEH-CHAWL
HAH-AH-RETZ

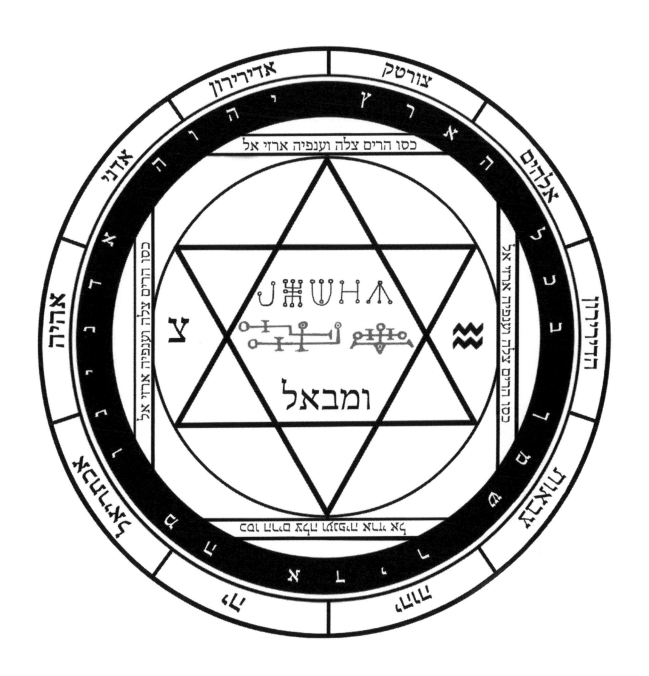

Umabel

OOM-AB-ELL

The Powers of Yahahel

To Obtain Wisdom and Knowledge

When you need to obtain wisdom on a particular subject, call on this angel. You may discover knew knowledge related to your question, or you may simply obtain grater clarity. This power is especially effective if you feel you are in a rut and you are looking for a new direction in life.

To Keep Secrets

This angel can help secrets to remain secret. If you are working on something that you want to remain hidden, call on this angel to help. You can keep things secret from everybody, or a specific person or a group of people. This power can be used to hide trade secrets, affairs, plans and anything else you want to remain hidden. A second way to use this power is to compel somebody else to keep your secret. If, for example, somebody you know sees you in a place that you shouldn't be, you can use this angel to silence them.

To Keep a Low Profile

There are times when you want your actions to remain unnoticed. If you call on this angel, you can go about your life without people taking much notice of what you are doing. This is also an excellent angel to call on when there is violence in your neighborhood and you wish to be inconspicuous.

Pronounced: YAH-AH-ELL

Invocation (Psalm 24:5)

YEE-SAH VEH-RAH-CHAH
MAY-ATE
EE-AH-OH-EH
OOTZ DEH-KAH
MAY-EH-LOW-HAY
YEESH-AWE

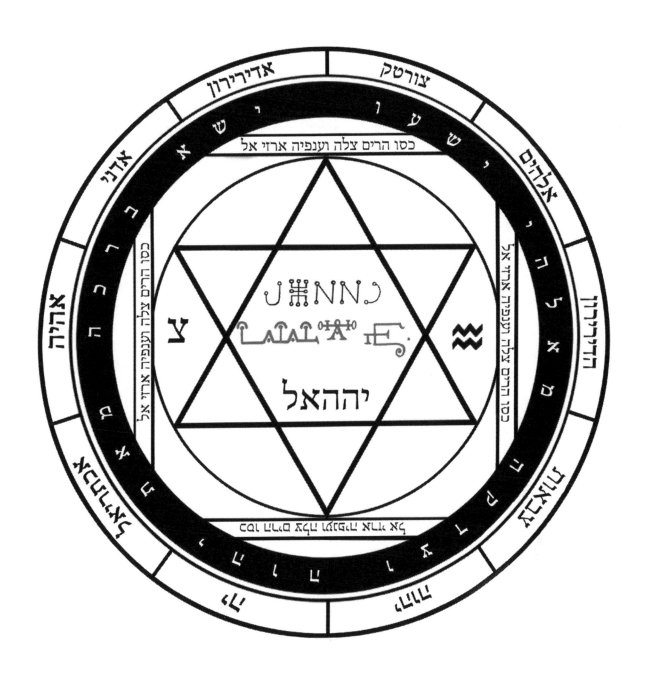

Yahahel

YAH-AH-ELL

The Powers of Anuel

Protect Your Business

When you have built up your business, you need to protect it from competition and unexpected disasters. Call on this angel when things are going well to ensure that they stay that way.

Make Good Financial Deals

When you are buying or selling a car, house or business, call on this angel to make sure you get the best deal. This works best when you know what deal you want to make and who you are making it with.

Pronounced: AH-NOO-ELL

Invocation (Psalm 37:4)

VEH-HE-TEH-AH-NAHG
AHL EE-AH-OH-EH
VEH-YEE-TEN
LEH-CHAH
MEESH-AH-LAWT
LEE-BECH-AH

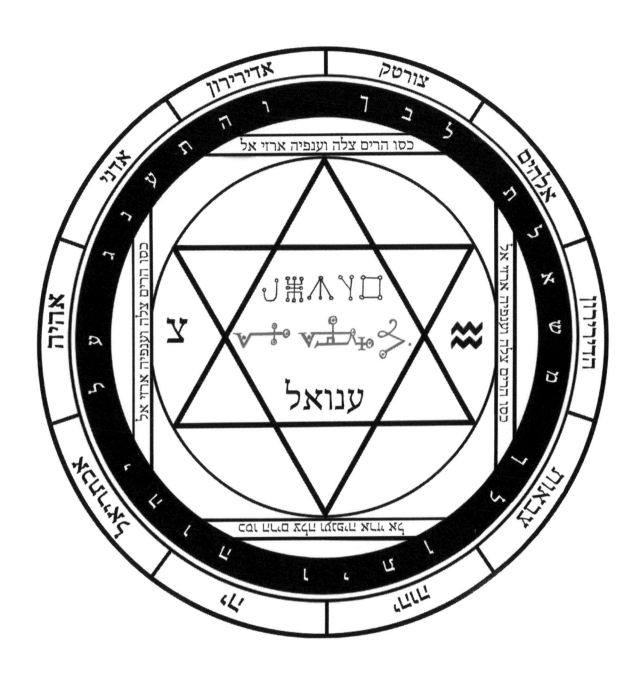

Anuel

AH-NOO-ELL

The Powers of Machiel

To Make You Write Well

There are many angels connected to writing, but call on this angel when you want the willpower to write often and well. The angel will inspire you with good ideas, but will also help you to overcome procrastination.

To Become a Popular Writer

This angel is a gift to writers and helps to make you popular. Call on this angel to help build your audience, so that readers like your work and remember your name.

Prowess in Marketing

The written word is incredibly important when you are marketing anything. Whether you are writing a letter to ask for a job, putting up a notice outside your coffee shop, or promoting your product or profession, this is the angel that will ensure you do a good job of selling yourself.

Pronounced: MAH-CHEE-ELL

Invocation (Psalm 30:10)

SHEM-AH EE-AH-OH-EH
VEH-CHAW-NAY-NEE
EE-AH-OH-EH
HEH-YEH AWE-ZAYR LEE

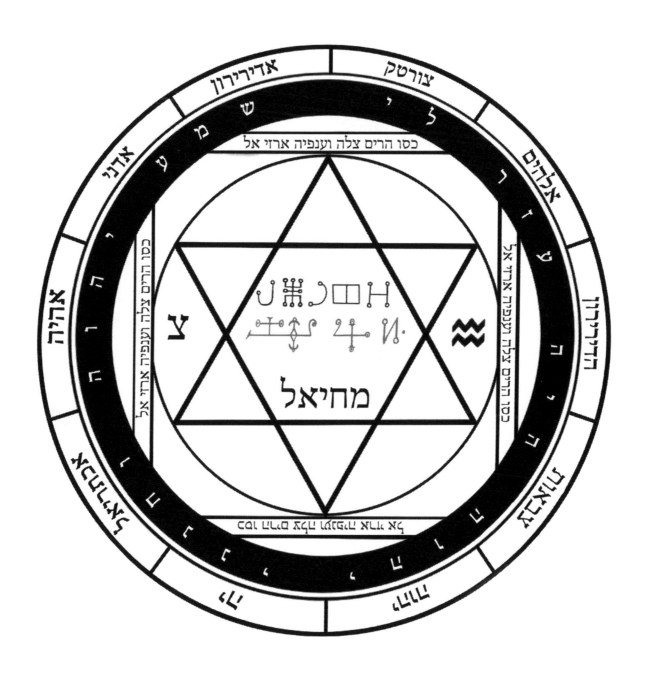

Machiel

MAH-CHEE-ELL

The Powers of Damebiah

The Power to Bring Business Success

This angel will not make a bad business thrive, but if you are making efforts to start a business or improve an existing business, do not miss the opportunities provided by Damebiah. This angel being success by guiding your actions and uncovering opportunities that you may not have seen, helping you make wise decisions that get your business to thrive.

The Power to Uncover Business Ideas

If you are already in business you may be seeking a new direction, or you may be looking to start a new business. If you need ideas to set your business aside from the competition, this angel will help. You will find that new ideas come to you more easily, and you will get a better sense of an idea's long-term potential. Without new ideas, business dies, so this is an extremely potent angelic power.

Pronounced: DAM-EH-BEE-AH

Invocation Psalm (90:13)

SHOO-VAH EE-AH-OH-EH
AHD MAH-TIE
VEH-HEEN-ACH-EM
AHL AH-VAH-DEH-CHAH

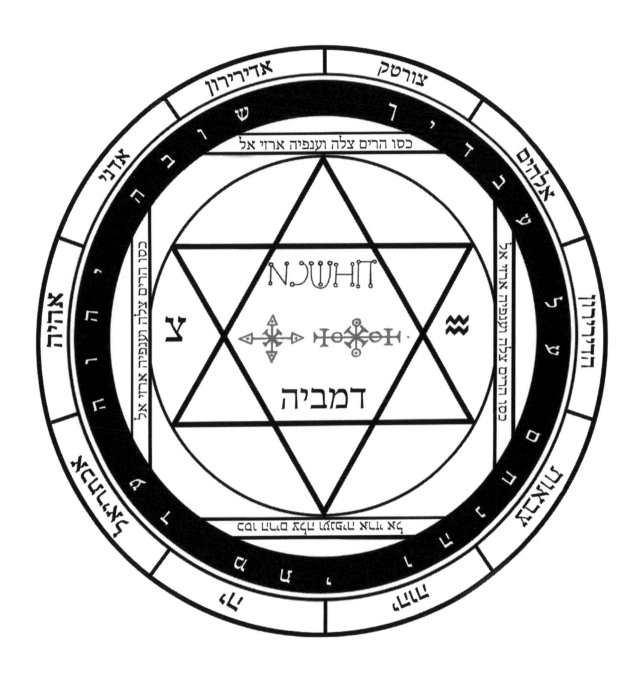

Damebiah

DAM-EH-BEE-AH

The Powers of Menakel

The Power to Find Lost Items

This angel can recover items thought to be lost, in seemingly miraculous ways. When calling on this angel, somebody else may bring the lost item to you, but it may also be up to you to find what has gone missing. Trust your intuition, and if you get any hunches, follow them. Once the item is found, you should still continue the ritual for the required number of days, but instead of asking for the item to be found, simply replace your request with thanks to the angel.

The Power to Obtain Clear Thought

When your mind is feeling confused or slow, when you are overwhelmed with options, call on this angel to clear your thoughts. The angel can be used simply to reset your normal state of mind after an ordeal, or to keep your thoughts clear during a stressful or demanding time.

The Power to Sleep Well

If you do not sleep well, call on this angel to help. Your sleep may improve immediately, or you may get nudges from your intuition, suggesting changes you can make that would aid your sleep. If you experience nightmares, this angel can bring them to a stop.

Pronounced: MEN-AH-KELL

Invocation (Psalm 87:2)

AWE-HAYV EE-AH-OH-EH
SHAH-AH-RAY TZEE-EE-AWN
MEE-KAWL MEESH-KEH-NAUGHT
YAH-AH-KAWV

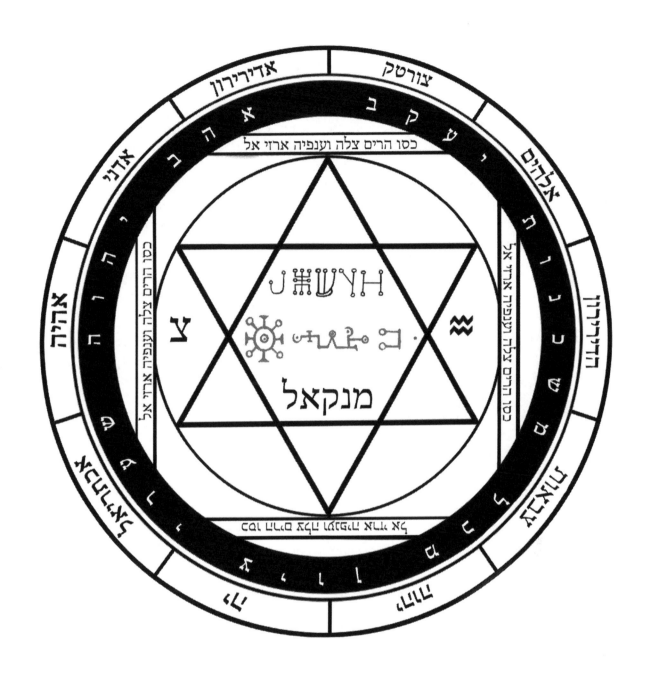

Menakel

MEN-AH-KELL

The Powers of Iyahel

The Power to Increase Fame

When you already have some degree of fame, this angel can increase your fame dramatically. You do not need to be famous in the sense of a celebrity. So long as you are well-known within certain circles, you can use this angel. Many public speakers, performers, writers and others use this angel to increase the number of people who know about them. Note that this angel works to increase fame by making you more well known, but it will not necessarily make you more liked. Consider this when wording your request, and phrase it carefully, to ensure you get positive fame rather than notoriety. Unless notoriety is what you want.

The Power to Stay Strong During Adversity

There are some situations we simply can't prevent. When a relative or friend is dying of incurable disease, when we are forced to move home, when a relationship breaks down beyond repair – this is when you call on Iyahel. If you are faced with unavoidable adversity, this angel will give you the strength to get through the coming weeks and months without being damaged or exhausted.

The Power to Break Free When Stuck

There are many times when people say they feel 'stuck', because their life or relationships are not developing as hoped, or because they simply don't know what to do next. In magickal terms, you want to 'open the road'. This means that you call on the angel to reveal a variety of new possibilities so that you can break free from feeling stuck.

Pronounced: EE-AH-ELL

Invocation (Psalm 18:46)

CHAY EE-AH-OH-EH
OO-VAH-ROOCH
TZAW-REE
VEH-VAH-ROOM
ELL-AWE-HAY
YEESH-EE

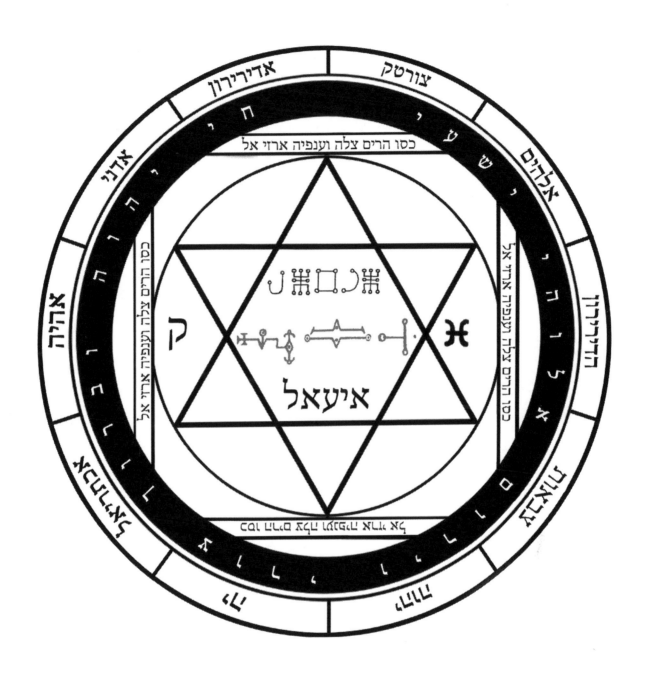

Iyahel

EE-AH-ELL

The Powers of Chavuiah

The Power to Recover from Disease

Although you can use this angel when you are unwell, the best results come when you have already begun to recover. When a long recovery is expected, this angel will speed up the recovery considerably.

The Power to Increase Love

This angel can increase feelings of genuine love. You should not use this to generate passion or exciting love, but to increase warm, ongoing love within a family, or in a relationship. It is best to use this angel when there is already love there, but you want the love to increase. This can help relationships to last, and families to be peaceful. It can also be used within strained friendships, to ensure that each party remembers the love they have for one another.

Pronounced: CHAH-VOO-EE-AH

Invocation (Psalm 132:13)

KEY VAH-CHAHR
EE-AH-OH-EH
BEH-TZEE-YAWN
EE-VAH
LEH-MAW-SHAHV LAW

Chavuiah

CHAH-VOO-EE-AH

The Powers of Raahel

Discover a Thief

When something goes missing and you suspect a thief, there is rarely anything you can do. Call on this angel, and you will find out who stole from you. The revelation may come in the form of insight or confession, or the person may simply be caught by the police.

Win a Financial Legal Action

If you are involved in a legal action that involves money or an inheritance, call on this angel to get the decision to fall in your favor.

Increase Fame and Reputation

Whether you are starting out on a new venture or seeking more popularity, this angel can bring you more fame. If you don't need fame, the angel can help to establish your good reputation.

Pronounced: RAH-AH-ELL

Invocation (Psalm 119:145)

KAH-RAH-TEE VEH-CHAWL
LEV AH-NAY-NEE
EE-AH-OH-EH
CHOO-KECH-AH
ETZ-AWE-RAH

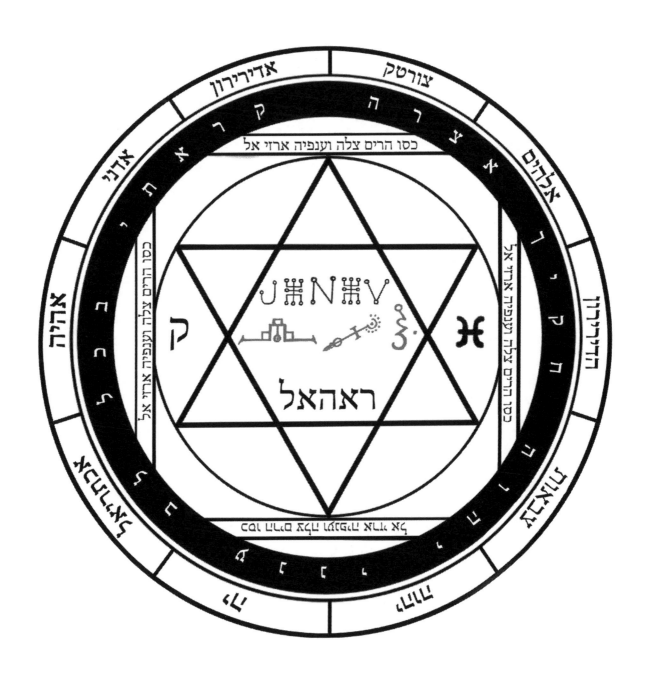

Raahel

RAH-AH-ELL

The Powers of Yabamiah

The Power to Recover

There are times when you may feel you need a break from life, but you don't have the time or space to recover. Call on this angel. Sometimes the angel will respond by creating a space in your life for you to recover, and at others times it will simply give you more strength to recover from within.

The Power to Find Inner Harmony

People sometimes seek inner harmony when everything is falling apart around them. Others seek inner harmony when everything they desire is falling into place, because they recognize this is also a time to appreciate and enjoy the results that have been obtained. This angel can bring you inner harmony, which means you will find peace and stability in your emotions, whatever is happening in the world around you.

Pronounced: YAH-BAH-ME-AH

Invocation (Psalm 145:17)

TZAH-DEEK EE-AH-OH-EH
BEH-CHAWL
DEH-RACH-AHV
VEH-CHAH-SEED
BEH-CHAWL
MAH-AH-SAHV

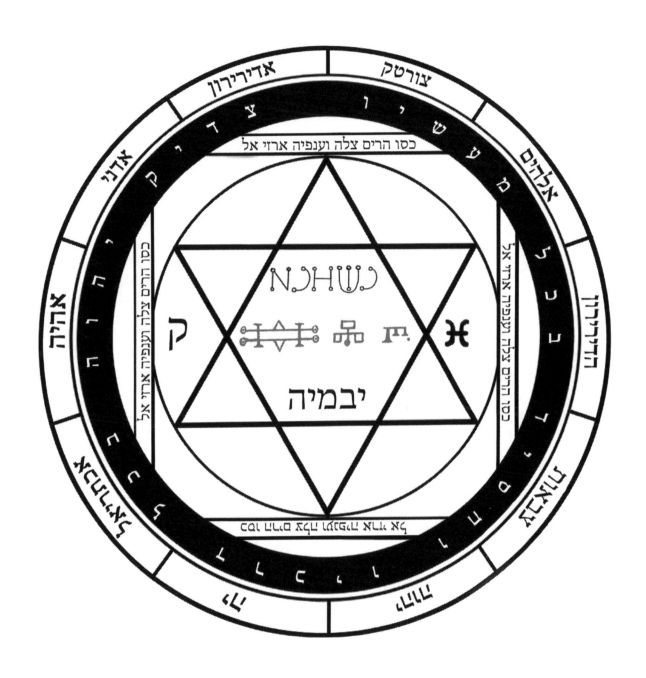

Yabamiah

YAH-BAH-ME-AH

The Powers of Hayiel

To Repel Curses

If you suspect, or know, that you are cursed, call on this angel to repel the evil. If you are certain that somebody specific has cursed you, name that person when you talk to the angel. Otherwise, ask that all curses aimed at you be repelled.

To Obtain Energy After a Draining Time

Whether you have been ill, over-worked or drained in any other way, this angel can give you your energy back. This is not a form of healing, but is simply a way for you to connect with your own inner light when it has been shut out by exhaustion and despair.

To Be Brave with Your Talents

If you suspect that your talents could take you much further than they have, you may need more courage to put your dreams into action. Call on this angel to give you the bravery required to make your talents shine in the world.

Greater Control with Magick

When you are performing any occult work, from this book or any other, you can call on this angel to give you more control. That is, you can ask the angel to increase your magickal skills, so that all your magick, or a particular working, is more effective. Some people believe this is the first request you should make of any angel.

Pronounced: HAH-YEE-ELL

Invocation Psalm (121:5)

EE-AH-OH-EH
SHAW-MEH-RECH-AH
EE-AH-OH-EH
TZEE-LEH-CHAH
AHL YAHD
YEH-MEEN-EH-CHAH

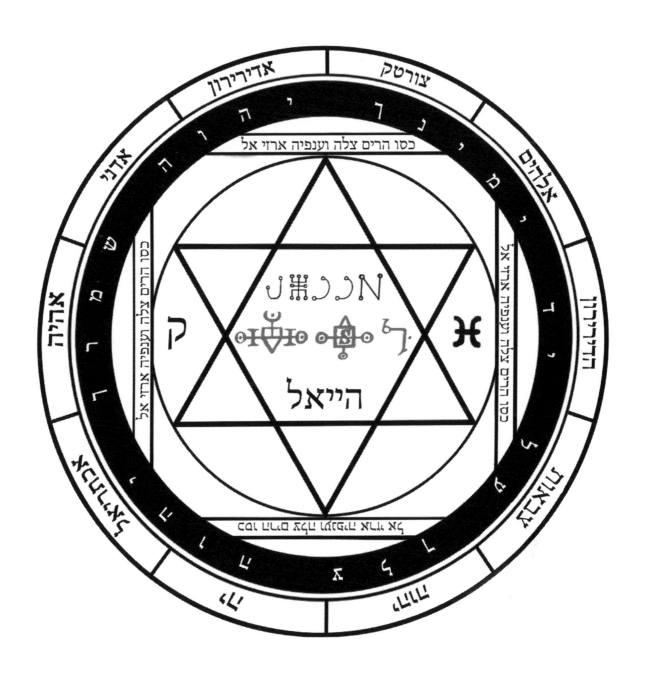

Hayiel

HAH-YEE-ELL

The Powers of Mumiah

To See a Project Through to Completion

It is easy to start a project, but difficult to see it through to the end. Whether you're seeking love, working on your art or trying to buy a house, a task can often feel so overwhelming that you want to give up. If you are certain that the project will benefit you, calling on this angel will help you see the project through to completion and may even speed up the process.

Protection When Doing Magick

The magick in this book is safe, but if you are ever tempted to work with demons, servitors, random spells or other techniques, you can call on this angel to protect you while you experiment.

To Expand Pleasure Through Sharing

When you share any magick, or any pleasure, you will find that your pleasure and gratitude increases. By calling on this angel, you will ensure that any time you share your love, enjoyment, humor, wealth or magickal power, you are rewarded many times over.

Pronounced: MOOM-EE-AH

Invocation (Psalm 131:3)

YAH-CHAYL
YEES-RAH-ELL
EL EE-AH-OH-EH
MAY-AH-TAH
VEH-AHD AWE-LAHM

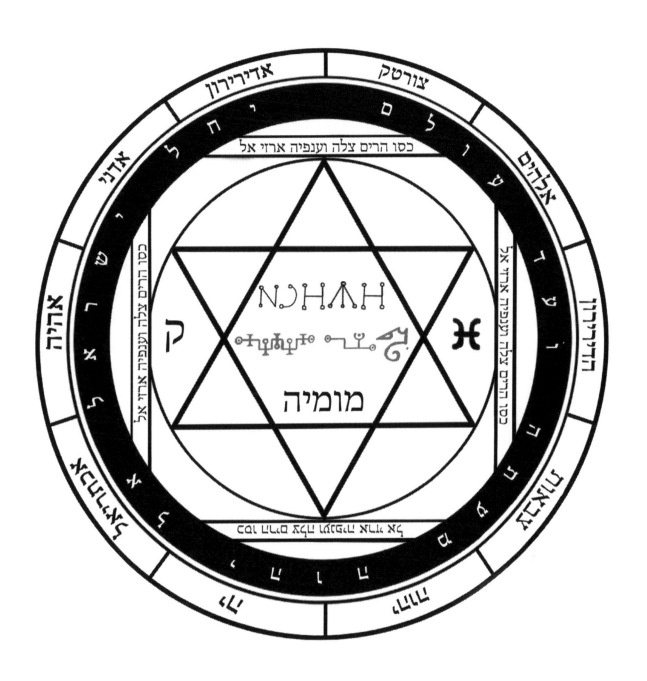

Mumiah

MOOM-EE-AH

The Act of Choosing

How do you choose the best angel to work with? The first thing to do is know what you really want. Many people immediately think they want more money, and do magick to solve that problem. If you take the time to think about what you really want, it may be something unexpected. I have often had people come to me for magickal help, and after some thought they've realized that what they really want is more love, peace or creativity.

There's nothing wrong with wanting more money. If you want to be more successful, or if you want your business to thrive, the angels will be willing to help. The angels do not judge or determine whether or not your cause is worthy. All they look at is the nature of your desire. If your desire is heartfelt, and comes from a genuine longing for change, the angels will give you what you want.

The best results, of course, come when you choose the right angels for the job, and sometimes that will mean breaking your problem down into stages. Imagine you are being attacked by a cruel enemy. You may want to perform an eleven-day ritual to weaken that enemy. You could then perform an eleven-day ritual to ensure that you are seen by other people in a good light. You could follow this up with a ritual to stop your enemy completely, with another ritual to ensure you recover from any damage that was done. Although this may seem long-winded, taking a lot of time to achieve, it is the best way to get results when faced with a large or enduring problem.

If you are trying to build business success, you should look at all the angelic powers that can assist you, and develop a plan for using them in succession, to gradually build your success. This is more effective than just doing one prosperity ritual and hoping for the best.

With that said, often all you need is one well-chosen angel and you will get the job done.

Sometimes, people want to use more than one angel at once. If there is a real emergency and you need help from several angels at once, you can do this, but consider that it might be better to put your trust in one angel, than to blast the problem with magick because you're afraid it won't work.

If you do use more than one angel on a single problem at the same time, you should perform the ritual with your request for one angel, finish it, and then repeat the entire process for the next angel on the same day. Ideally, you should break your problem down into smaller stages, and work on each stage in sequence.

I explained this to a group of people some time ago, and there were a few groans of disappointment. People just wanted to do all the magick at once. Doing four eleven-day rituals was going to take months, they said. I agreed, but pointed out that months of good magick is better than one attempt that fails because it has not been well thought out. So you are free to use several angels at the same time, on the same problem, or on different problems, but make sure you have thought deeply about your problem and the results you want.

Before you choose your angel, you should know that the powers described in this book are not the same powers you might find listed elsewhere. Traditionally, these angels are ascribed many powers that may differ from those listed in this book.

These angels have been known for a long, long time, and there are many different ways of using them. You can look online and find all sorts of 'abilities' that are attributed to them. You can track down the oldest source texts and see that the descriptions are quite different. You can buy lots of modern books that will say different things altogether. And then when you evoke the angels, you find out something else entirely.

The powers listed in this book are taken from decades of direct work with these angels, with our initial work being based on the best source text we could find (which is not widely available online). That doesn't mean you can't try using the angels to achieve results that aren't listed here, but when starting out, the listed powers give you a good insight into the angel's general nature.

You should, however, spend some time reading through the powers, and then there is a brief ritual you can perform to sense the angel's powers more directly. If an angel interests you, gaze at its sigil for a while, and let your focus rest on the angel's seal. This is the collection of lines that are at the very center of the sigil. You can think of this as a gateway to the angel. When you look at those lines you are not looking at shapes, but looking through into another space where the angel resides. When you have let your eyes settle on the image, consider your problem or the challenge you face, and try to imagine this angel helping you. Imagine what might happen if you called on this angel. Do not try to direct your thoughts, but allow feelings to arise. You may get the slightest sensation, or feel an immense rush of power. The scale of the feeling is not important. What matters is the quality of the feeling. If the angel feels like it might be able to help, you have made your choice. If you feel nothing immediately, allow some time to pass and gaze again. You may find that you get a better intuition about each angel as you continue to gaze at the sigils.

When performing magick, it is not your job to decide how the result will manifest. Although angelic magick can be more direct and precise than most magick, you still need to leave room for manifestation to occur. So if you want to silence an enemy, you don't need to specify how they will be silenced. You shouldn't ask the angel to make sure the enemy leaves town, because that's too specific. Instead, make your request sincerely, and let the angel handle the details.

Getting Involved with Your Magick

To get magick working you need to do two things. You need to keep working in the real-world to make the results come about, and you need to let go of Lust For Result. This chapter will look at the real-world work, and the next chapter will look at Lust For Result.

I had a friend who said that if magick requires people to put in real-world effort, it was probably just the real-world effort that made a difference. I used to think the same, but I have seen astonishing things happen when you put in a little more work.

When you perform magick, you are making a pact with reality. You are asking reality to promise you a result, and you are promising to live with that result.

If you are serious about getting a result, you should do everything you can to make the result come about. The more effort you put into a situation in the real world, the more the magick works. The beautiful thing about this is that if you double your efforts, magick works ten times harder for you. If you triple your efforts, magick works a hundred times harder. These aren't exact numbers, but you get the idea.

I should say that sometimes, extra effort isn't required, for certain types of working. If you're doing a ritual from *Magickal Cashbook*, for example, then you're trying to make money appear out of the blue. There's not much you can do in the real world other than let go of your Lust For Result and allow the manifestation to occur in whatever way it wants.

On the other hand, if you're doing a working to increase sales in your shop, for example, there's plenty you could do to help. When you're doing magick to increase sales, this is the time to start making changes to your advertising, to your store's layout, to the products you stock or whatever else occurs to you. If you work for an employer, and you want a promotion or a better job, there are hundreds of ways to increase your abilities and potential, rather than sitting back and hoping. By stirring up the potential for change, you give magick many more ways to manifest. This is especially true when performing angelic magick.

This doesn't just mean working harder, but breaking a goal down into several stages. If you want to become a painter, then you should do magick to improve your skills, do magick to get people to like your work, do magick to get your first exhibition and sales, and then do magick to improve your popularity. This is better than just doing one ritual to make you a famous artist.

I know a lot of actors, and although some have a small degree of fame, most of the actors I know are 'jobbing' actors, who work in theatre and smaller TV productions. That's where most of the work is, and to make a living at that level is seen as a major achievement. I'm proud of them and they are fairly proud of themselves. Most actors never even make it that far, so it's a good result. Many of these actors got where they are by using magick. But they used far more than magick. Every one of them had trained, rehearsed, auditioned and trained again, for years, ensuring they were the best possible actors they could be. They made sure they were in the right place at the right time, and they ensured that every moment they had spare was spent on seeing theatre shows, networking and getting involved with the acting scene. By being prepared, they were making sure they could respond when the magick kicked in. It doesn't always happen that way.

I've had many actors ask me for help, and my first advice to them is to move to LA, New York, Vancouver, London or a similar city. Once they are willing to do that, magick can work wonders. If they try to do magick in a town where there's no acting work, though, then it's probably a waste of time. It may seem like harsh advice, but this is what I mean by commitment. (If your ambition is only local, then I support that, but many people dream of Hollywood and hope they'll be discovered in a small English village.)

I knew an actor who desperately wanted to succeed, but he wanted the success first and the learning and hard work afterwards. This may sound like insanity, but you'd be surprised at how often this approach is the case. People start bands without learning to play guitar. People write novels without reading enough novels to know how they're written. People want to be wealthy without understanding how money works or even how to spend it well.

This actor came to me for magickal advice, and I said I'd give him what he needed when he'd done everything else that he could do to get the job. To get the role he wanted he needed several new acting skills and a certain physique - so I told him to get out there and do the hard work, and then we could use magick when it mattered. If you do magick without doing the real-world work, it's wasted magick, I said.

Unfortunately, he didn't listen to me. He used the magick that he already knew (from many years of being friends with me) to get an audition. And he worked hard at getting that audition. Against the odds, he managed to get an audition. That was a stunning piece of magickal work, because he didn't even have an agent. He used magick to achieve the impossible. But it was a mistake. When he got to the audition, he didn't have the right skills or physique and was not the best actor he could be. He failed the audition.

Magick can give you what you want, but you need to make sure you are ready for the result and ready to respond to the result.

Making a pact means doing your share of the work. If you're trying to avoid an enemy, you shouldn't do magick to avoid the enemy and then confront your enemy at their front door. If you're doing magick to increase business success, make sure you're ready to respond to new developments.

When you get involved with the result you want to see, the angels see your sincerity and respond with magick.

The Art of Letting Go

When you perform magick, you are advised not to lust for results. Putting in real-world effort is important, but letting go of results is vital for them to manifest. To let go of the magickal result, you need to show a little confidence in your magick. This means that you don't constantly check up on the magick or count the days since you finished your ritual. The less you rush the magick, the faster it works.

This doesn't mean you have to believe or pray or hope for the magick to work, but it means you have to act as though you expect the result to manifest. This expectation should have the same level of calm that you feel when stepping out of your house to get into your car. You don't hope that your car is there, or pray that it hasn't been stolen. You expect it to be there. So you grab your keys and head to the car because you assume it will be there. For some people, when they perform magick, they head to the car without picking up their keys, so to speak.

All you're trying to achieve is a casual confidence that magick works. This is why I suggest to beginners that they work on attracting small changes. When people use some basic protection magick, or attract a small amount of money, they see a result, and their confidence increases. Building on this, they are soon able to work miracles. All it requires is a casual state of mind.

To achieve this state of mind, you should perform the magick with confidence and serious intent, but when the magick is done, know that you have handed the magick over to another power. It's that simple. Whatever entity you have summoned *will* do the work. You need to remember this. You have asked the angel to help, and you have done so in a state of magickal authority. The least you can do is act as though you expect the angel to do what it has been asked to do.

Of course, if you have a burning desire, it's difficult to forget about the result you want, but rather than worrying about the magick or how it may manifest, think about what you can do to make the result come about. When you find yourself pondering the magick, simply let yourself feel pleasure as though the result has already been obtained. It's mental trickery, but it goes a long way to unlocking the inner blockages that hold back the magick.

The magick I present in my books is so powerful that some people report results within seconds. At other times, great patience is required. Whatever happens, keep working on the problem in the real world, and know that magick will find a way.

Remember that you are handing the problem over to the angels, at the same time as committing to work on the problem in the real world. When doing magick, focus on your magick. When working in the real world, focus on the real world and let the magick take care of itself.

Doing Magick for Others

When you discover that magick works, you may find that you want to perform magick for others. You can do so, without even asking for their permission, but you should take great care.

If somebody is ill, there is little harm in performing a ritual to make them well. All you need to do is guide your request to the angel, asking for healing for the other named party. You can communicate how they have suffered, and how the magick will help them, but you should also mention how good it will make you feel if the magick works. Do not try to be pious. The angels just want to know what you really feel. If helping somebody is going to make you feel good, let the angels know.

This technique can be applied to any angelic power. You can use the powers to increase the prosperity of those you care about, protect loved ones from enemies, or keep somebody's job safe. You should be cautious, though, because what you think somebody wants may not be what *they* want. Somebody may swear blind that they want their spouse to leave the house for ever, but what they really want is more love. Somebody may tell you they are desperate for a new job, but what they really want is an early retirement.

If you are certain you know what the person wants, you can go ahead and perform the magick, but you should add this statement to your request, 'In accordance with the will of....' Here you name the person you are trying to help. This means that the magick will only work if it fits in with the deepest desires of the person you are trying to help.

The other option is to ask the person in question if they want magickal help, but this is rarely wise. Many people are horrified by the thought of magick, even angelic magick, and others may be insulted by your offer of help. Your initial delight in the power to help others can be soured with a few reactive words. At other times, people will be overjoyed that you made the offer. Take the time to consider the person you know carefully, before discussing magick with them.

There are great benefits in performing magick for others. You can perform these rituals alongside your own, and this helps you to build relationships with more angels. The more magick you do – when the need is sincere – the better you become at doing magick.

When Magick Works

The magick in this book works easily for most people, but if you find it difficult, *The Gallery of Magick* website blog contains many FAQs, along with advice and practical information that is updated on a regular basis.

www.galleryofmagick.com

The Gallery of Magick Facebook page will also keep you up to date.

If you have an interest in developing your magick further, there are many texts that can assist you. *The Angels of Alchemy* works with 42 angels, to obtain personal transformation. *The 72 Sigils of Power*, by Zanna Blaise, covers Contemplation Magic (for insight and wisdom) and Results Magic (for changing the world around you). Zanna is also the author of *The Angels of Love*, which uses a tasking method with six angels to heal relationships, or to attract a soulmate.

Words of Power and *The Greater Words of Power* present an extremely simple ritual practice, for bringing about change in yourself and others, as well as directing and attracting changed circumstances.

For those seeking more money, *Magickal Cashbook* uses a ritual to attract small bursts of money out of the blue, and works best when you are not desperate, but when you can approach the magick with a sense of enjoyment and pleasure. *Magickal Riches* is more comprehensive, with rituals for everything from gambling to sales, with a master ritual to oversee magickal income. For the more ambitious, *Wealth Magick* contains a complex set of rituals for earning money by building a career. For those still trying to find their feet, there is *The Magickal Job Seeker*.

Magickal Protection contains rituals that can be directed at specific problems, as well as a daily practice called The Sword Banishing, which is one of our most popular and effective rituals. For those who cannot find peace through protection there is *Magickal Attack*, by Gordon Winterfield. Dark magick is not to everybody's taste, but this is a highly moral approach that puts the emphasis on using authority to restore peace.

Magickal Seduction is a text that looks at attracting others by using magick to amplify your attractive qualities, rather than through deception. *Adventures in Sex Magick* is a more specialized text, for those open minded enough to explore this somewhat extreme form of magick.

The Master Works of Chaos Magick by Adam Blackthorne is an overview of self-directed and creative magick, which also includes a section covering the Olympic Spirits. *Magickal Servitors* takes another aspect of Chaos Magick and updates it into a modern, workable method.

Damon Brand

www.galleryofmagick.com

Appendix A: The Master Ritual Simplified

Face East.

Place the Shem Talisman before you.

> This is the beginning. I open the way.

Make the opening gesture.

Gaze at the Shem Talisman, then keep your eyes on the central triangle as you say:

> I call on the inner world to know that this is my will.
>
> NAH-KAH EE-AH-OH-EH
> NAH-KAH EE-AH-OH-EH
> NAH-KAH EE-AH-OH-EH

Picture the following images as clearly as you can, as you say:

> I pass through the arch of stone.
> I walk through a field of golden corn.
> I am warmed by fire of the sun.
> I am cooled by water of the ocean.
> I am steady on the firm earth.
> I breathe a sweet breeze.
> I feel the weight of the earth beneath me.

Ask these questions of yourself, out loud, but do not attempt to answer them in any way:

> I ask, how did I come to be at peace?
> I ask, how did I let go of fear?
> I ask, how did I learn to manifest my dreams?

Imagine an orange glow on your left. Imagine a purple glow on your right. Imagine these lights for just a few moments.

Make sure the angelic sigil is before you. If you need to flip to a new page in the book, you no longer need to see the Shem Talisman.

Scan your eyes over the letters in the square of your chosen sigil, as discussed earlier.

Say:

I call on thee, Arzel (ARE-ZELL)* in the East,
to connect me to the secret angels of the universe.

Kosu hariym tzilah va'anafeha arzey-El
(KOH-SUE HAH-REE-EEM TZIL-AH VAH-ANNA-FEHA ARE-ZELL)

ARE-ZELL*, ARE-ZELL*, ARE-ZELL*

ARZ-ALE*, ARZ-ALE*, ARZ-ALE*

ARE-ZAY-ELL*, ARE-ZAY-ELL*, ARE-ZAY-ELL*

I call on thee, Raziel (RAH-ZEE-ELL*) in the East
to make me heard by the secret angels of the universe.

RAH-ZEE-ELL*, RAH-ZEE-ELL*, RAH-ZEE-ELL*

VAH-HAH-DEH-REH-CHAH
TZ-LAH
REH-CHAB
AL-DEH-BAR-EH-MET
VAY-AHN-VAH-TZAY-DECK
VAY-TORE-AY-CHAR
NAW-RAH-AUGHT
YEH-ME-NAY-CHAH

Oh Raziel (RAH-ZEE-ELL*),
let my voice be heard by the
great angel _____ *
I seal this command with the
word of power
AH-RAH-REE-TAH

Visually scan the letters of the Invocation Chant in the black circle, in an anti-clockwise direction.

Speak The Invocation Chant for your chosen angel.

Glance at the sigil and Sing the Angel's name three times:

_____ *, _____ *, _____ *

Speak Your Request to The Angel:

I call on thee, powerful ___ *, who ……..

…………

I seal this command with the word of power:
AH-RAH-REE-TAH

As you angels have come in peace, go in peace. It is done.

Made in the USA
Lexington, KY
20 October 2016